How to Be Queen of the Universe

by Tahira Chloe Mahdi

Edited and Illustrated by
Club Miss

A Dream Come True
from

Tuff Crowd Conglomerate

How to Be Queen of the Universe

Text and illustrations copyright © 2005 by Tahira Chloe Mahdi. All rights reserved. No part of this book may be reproduced or transmitted in any form or by any means except for brief quotes.
Publisher may be contacted for permission.

All quotations remain the intellectual property of their respective originators. However, the author of this book asserts a claim of copyright for this particular compilation of information, material and quotations and the unique arrangement of this work.

Published by Tuff Crowd Conglomerate, LLC.

ISBN-13: 978-0-9740591-1-2
ISBN-10: 0-9740591-1-0

For information, contact Tuff Crowd Conglomerate, LLC (Media, Publishing, and Entertainment) at:
www.tuffcrowd.com

Printed in the United States

First Edition

To the best of the author/publisher's knowledge, use of all quotes herein falls under "fair use". Quotes included are for the purpose of research and scholarship in the spirit of enriching and uplifting a universal goodwill toward human beings, not for competition in or impairment of any literary or entertainment markets.

Inclusion of a quote does not mean that its author or originator endorses this book or the author of this book, nor does it mean that the author of this book endorses all work by the authors of the quotes included. Extensive research was done to ensure the accuracy of the included quotes; however, neither the author nor the publisher of this book can be held responsible for any errors in quotations or attributions.

Dedication

This one's for me... 'cause I definitely need it.

Also dedicated to the ladies of *Club Miss*:
Miss Demeanor, Miss Fit, and Miss Understood;
in association with "Butterfly on the Wall"
Entertainment and "Stained Dress" Productions;
funded in part by "Got My Drink" Promotions...

For every woman, everywhere.

Author's Note

This book was designed with wishes for your happiness and the beautiful sound of your laughter. The information and inspiration brought to you from this particular channel, is but one of many available to you if you are ready to let go of pain and unhappiness. Men and women all over the United States have also taken the time to contribute their feelings and thoughts to this project in hopes that we can all improve the quality of our lives. I am thankful for their support and love. I hope that you are as well.

If you read a suggestion in this book that makes you say, "That wouldn't work for me," consider this: You could be right. But wouldn't you rather be HAPPY? If you are ready to be HAPPY rather than simply being correct about the fact that you have no control over a miserable situation... Tell yourself, "I am ready to receive the goodness of Life." Say your prayers and keep in mind that in all situations, you must seek the Highest Power (God) first. By doing so, this book will only bring you what you need – the goodness that God has for you and tons of fun! Don't you deserve it?

This book is, above all, for entertainment purposes - to lift your spirits. It is not meant to be a substitute for spiritual guidance you already know that you need, a psychiatrist you may need to see or counseling you may need to get. However, I sincerely hope that you will choose my book and others like it - but the Highest Power, especially - over the drugs being pushed to you on television.

I'm not a doctor and you are old enough to think for yourself. So, why am I qualified to give such advice?

I've seen the light... Watched it shine down on me... I'm gonna spread my wings, yeah... and I'm gonna tell all I see. These happy feelin's... I'll spread them all over the world... from deep in my soul. - Maze featuring Frankie Beverly, "Happy Feelin's" (song)

In addition, I've included some of modern history's best proverbs and some of the greatest quotes from well-known figures all over the world, past and present. For example:

When I read great literature, great drama, speeches, or sermons, I feel that the human mind has not achieved anything greater than the ability to share feelings and thoughts through language. – James Earl Jones, actor

I reserve the right to take you from funny, to serious, to sarcastic, to slightly angry, to optimistic, to having just a smidgen of hope... all in the turning of a page. There are plenty of open spaces in this book. Use them to write in your own feelings about the topics explored. Let your mind wander, draw a picture... be my co-author!

Thank you for reading and I salute the Divinity within you!

Sincerely wishing you Love, Light and Laughter,
Tahira Chloe Mahdi

Contents

Assume the Position
10 Steps to Getting Started . . . 3
Being Queen . . . 5
Forget THEM . . . 6

Her Power
Your Power Source . . . 8
Getting Into the Role
    Names and Themes . . . 11
    The Royal Beauty Salon and Spa . . . 12
    The Queendom . . . 18
    Give to Yourself . . . 24

Her Grace
Being Queen . . . 27
Know the Difference: Queen/Witch . . . 28
Queen's Social Life . . . 33
Mirror, Mirror: Skin Problems . . . 35
Peace in Friendships . . . 38
Oh, the Drama!
    The Queen vs. The Drama Queen . . . 43

Her Majesty
Choosing Victory over Sympathy . . . 60
Wordplay: No way . . . 62
Whatcha Really Want . . . 64

Her Excellency
Current Job vs. Dream Job . . . 76
Your Career and Your Power Source . . . 77
Choose Your Own Attitude . . . 81

Inspiration, not Envy . . . 84
Make It Happen . . . 85
Sex and Your Career . . . 86
The Queen vs. The Peasant . . . 87

Her King
Intro . . . 90
10 Facts about Men . . . 92
The Single Queen
    Meeting His Royal Highness . . . 98
    Whatcha Really Want . . . 105
    Lost Art of Flirting . . . 107
    The Chase . . . 112
    The Bedroom War . . . 112
    Reality Check: Rape . . . 116
    Know the Difference: Serious/Screwing . . . 122
A Queen in Love
    Well-Meaning Actions That Screw Up . . . 124
    Know the Difference: Prize/Piece of Meat . . . 132
    Wordplay: Your way . . . 135
    Nobody's Business? . . . 138
    Trust . . . 140
    Wordplay: He say . . . 146
    Mirror, Mirror: Ego Trips . . . 156
    Know the Difference: Stay/Go . . . 162
    Wordplay: Can't stay . . . 168
    Mirror, Mirror: Entertainment . . . 170
    Whatcha Really Want . . . 178
    HIStory . . . 182

Her Highness
Diagnosis . . . 188
Know the Difference: Love Weight/Love Body . . . 194
Mirror, Mirror: Losing Weight . . . 196
On the Royal Menu . . . 200
The Whole World in Your Hands . . . 202
Mirror, Mirror: Vaginal Infections . . . 204

Share the Wealth (interviews with women)
The best thing about being a woman . . . 10
Confidence and arrogance . . . 25
Queens and drama queens . . . 41
Empowering through entertainment . . . 54
Mom's advice . . . 69
Treasured traditions . . . 74
Following dreams . . . 78
Being sexy . . . 110
Cheering up . . . 192
Good food . . . 198
Stress and illness . . . 207
Rules . . . 211

Kings Speak (interviews with men)
Models, movie stars and you . . . 14
Confident and arrogant women . . . 29
Queens and drama queens . . . 49
Flirting . . . 101
What women should get about men . . . 126
Mothering is smothering . . . 142
The other woman . . . 151
The perfect woman . . . 184

Try this! (Strategies for Happiness)
Great ways to feel attractive . . . 16
Release your past through song . . . 22
Fight road rage . . . 40
"All Hail the Queen" Jamboree . . . 53
Forgive . . . 68
180 for a day . . . 73
Hypnotize yourself . . . 83
Peace in your relationship . . . 130
Easy exercises . . . 193
Water for a week . . . 201
Queen Themes . . . 209

The Queen Takes On... (Do's and Don'ts)
Guilt . . . 20
Loneliness . . . 57
Critics . . . 66
The Overbearing Family . . . 71
Evil Coworkers . . . 88
The Man Who Doesn't Spend Enough Time . . . 149
The Cheating Lover . . . 160
The Ex . . . 176
Suicidal Thoughts . . . 190

Happily Ever After
About "Kings Speak" and the men interviewed . . . 214
About "Share the Wealth" / quotes on age . . . 216
Author's Thanks
About the Author

How to Be
Queen of the Universe

Assume the Position

10 Steps to Getting Started

1. Open your mind.

2. Lighten up! This is going to be fun!

3. Acknowledge the Highest Power. This is otherwise known as God or your idea of who or what God is. It is this power that connects and sustains every living thing. This is where your power and happiness comes from as Queen of the Universe.

4. Believe that you deserve to be and CAN be happy all of the time. Yes, that's right. ALL OF THE TIME. All you have to do is choose to be.

5. Think of all the traits that the Queen of the Universe should have. Begin to exhibit these traits at all times, behaving as if you were wearing the most glorious crown imaginable.

6. Expect nothing but the best that Life and Love have to offer.

7. Choose your words carefully as if everything you say is a law, a rule, or a command. Be careful with every utterance, statement and joke because as Queen of the Universe... what you say goes.

8. Have fun with this journey. It was designed out of

Love, especially for beautiful you.

9. Share what you learn with others, especially men and younger women.

10. Remember... "If you always do what you've always done, you'll always get what you've always gotten." In order to change a situation, we must change our behaviors and thoughts.

Ladies first, there's no time to rehearse... I'm Divine and my mind expands throughout the Universe. - Queen Latifah, "Ladies First" (song)

Being Queen of the Universe

It has nothing to do with:

-your skin color
-your hair texture
-your weight
-your height
-your past
-your level of education
-your love life (or lack of one)
-your family's status
-your neighborhood
-your religion
-your city
-your country
-your job (or lack of one)
-your bank statement (or lack of one)
-your marital status

A human being is part of the whole, called by us 'universe,' a part limited in time and space. He experiences himself, his thoughts and feelings, as something separate from the rest — a kind of optical delusion of consciousness. This delusion is a kind of prison for us, restricting us to our personal desires and to affection for a few persons nearest to us. Our task must be to free ourselves from this prison by widening our circle of compassion to embrace all living creatures and the whole of nature in its beauty. – Albert Einstein

Forget THEM

THEY are distorting your Divine image.

Fashion critics
Drug companies
Fast food industry
Snack food industry
Movies, music videos
Jealous people
Well-meaning relatives and friends
Plastic surgery enthusiasts
Insecure men
Our own scared selves

Every day, all women get subtle or not so subtle hints that we are not good enough just the way we are. THEY have us thinking that we should change our hair color, our skin tones, the way we choose to dress or the sizes of our body parts in order to be considered "beautiful".

It's nothing new; we're constantly being hit with the same brainwashing bunch of crap. THEY are trying to bring us to our knees! We have a tendency to fall victim every now and then to what THEY say. A woman's ethnicity, hair texture, weight, bank account, height, popularity, marital status, or geographical location doesn't guarantee her safety from THEM.

It's time to collectively tell THEM to kiss our already perfect butts!

Queens of the Universe don't play the blame game. We take responsibility for our own lives and everything that happens to us. We know that THEY can't do anything to us that we don't let THEM do.

Being Queen of the Universe is not about feeling superior to others. Instead, it is about recognizing yourself as an important, worthy person and encouraging others to do the same. Imagine a world full of people with positive self-images. Go on... imagine!

What you know you can't explain, but you feel it. You've felt it your entire life - that there's something wrong with the world. You don't know what it is, but it's there, like a splinter in your mind, driving you mad. – Morpheus, "The Matrix" (movie)

Her Power

Your Power Source

Demonstrate the Highest Power within you. In all your ways acknowledge it. It is through this power that *your* powers come. When we believe in ourselves and in the fact that we can be vessels for God's power, we can overcome anything. We show and prove to other people.

You are Queen of the Universe because you do the work of your Power Source. You allow your Power Source to work through you.

You make the whole Universe a better place in which to live by satisfying and fully utilizing your Power Source. Your personal pleasure comes secondary to your acceptance of this. Fortunately, staying in tune with your Power Source and maintaining that connection keeps you in the best possible situations and allows only the best things to come into your life. Remain in the practice of inviting Divine ideas to reign in your mind.

The Queen of the Universe knows that she can have anything she wants because her mind is just THAT powerful. However, she knows that relying on her basic human instincts 100% of the time can be very dangerous. This is where your Power Source comes in.

Your Power Source is not FOR you only.
It is for everyone.

Your Power Source is not IN you only.
It is in everyone.

It is your responsibility to allow that Power Source in everyone to work for your benefit.

QUEEN'S RULE: I AM NEVER TOO HIGH AND MIGHTY TO SEEK ANSWERS FROM GOD.

Share the Wealth

Question: What is the best thing about being a woman?

"The effect of my laughter when I'm flirting. I LOVE that! It makes me say, *I'm a girl*, and I love being a girl." - *Michelle*

"Being admired for our beauty, being mothers, and the feminine wiles. God blessed us with good ole Mother Wit!" - *Rebecca*

"The power we have over men. Oh, and wearing skirts, high-heels and sexy undies even if it's just to boost my spirits for the day. <giggle>" - *Tahira*

"The best thing about being a woman is our strength, love, and power." - *SasseeDiva*

"The ability to give life to a new generation." - *Terri*

"To be able to love everyone unconditionally. And sex... the feeling." - *Lola*

"Mama's baby, Daddy's maybe. No matter who the father may be, the child is definitely mom's. Also, women can have sex any and every day forever." - *Sunshine*

"We are blessed with the opportunity to give birth. Bringing a life into this world is one of the best gifts that women are given." - *Samantha*

Getting into the Role

Your Royal Alias

Need a little help getting into the Queen swing? Give yourself a royal alias. Go to the library or log onto the Internet for some fun research. Find names that have significant meanings, even in other languages. When you picture yourself on the Universal throne, picture Queen __(insert royal alias)__. Your current name may have a special meaning, so you can use that if you'd like. Now just throw "Her Majesty, Queen" in front of it and let your light shine!

Your Queen Theme

Every Queen deserves a crown and her own theme music. Pick one song or one hundred that help you feel empowered and at your best. No time for sad songs now; this is about encouraging yourself! Choose a song that makes you feel beautiful, happy and excited about life.

(See more about using music to remind you of your power on page 209.)

Step Into the Royal Beauty Salon and Spa

Skin Peel
Peel off the layers of criticism and other people's ignorant beliefs about you and your Life.

Body Wrap
Wrap yourself in Love! Picture it surrounding you like a most intimate hug. Shucks, couldn't ya use one?

Foot Massage
For the hard road you've walked. Take a load off your feet by giving your burdens to your Power Source. Your feet are renewed and ready for stepping up onto the throne.

Pedicure
Crossed the burning sands of love, haven't we? The spots hardened by your stupid ex-lovers are now soft again. Your feet feel perfect for when you're ready to cozy them up to someone worthy.

Manicure
You've been holding on to the wrong things. This will make it easier for you to release past indiscretions and let pain and guilt go.

Extra-Special Manicure with Hand Massage
Don't just give those tired hands a break; transform them! Are they used to working hard to make someone else rich? Now they can work to make YOU rich! Entrepreneur dreams? Go for it!

Deep Cleansing Facial
Get out all the ground-in lies that are make up ads and fashion magazine layouts. Feel the tingle of realiza-

tion that a magazine image is really no competition for the Queen of the Universe.

De-Stress Shampoo
Worry and anxiety are murder on hair. Lather the negativity right on outta there and step out with a fresh attitude on life.

Waxing
If you have to go through that much pain to pull something from yourself, pull away those memories of past hurts, regrets and hard lessons learned. (The actual hair on your body is *your* business.)

We ask ourselves, 'Who am I to be brilliant, gorgeous, talented, and fabulous?' Actually, who are you not to be? You are a child of God. Your playing small doesn't serve the world. There is nothing enlightened about shrinking so that other people won't feel insecure around you. We were born to make manifest the glory of God that is within us. - Nelson Mandela

KINGS SPEAK

Question: Should a woman strive to look like a model, movie star, or pop star? Why or why not? How can she know when she's taking it too far?

A man:
"No, because that look is ugly. She knows she's gone to far when no one's hollerin' [approaching her]."

Greg:
"Be comfortable in who you are. Every person that God put on this earth is beautiful; there are no ugly people. The biggest thing people should do is be healthy. Some people aren't as small as models, some are big-boned. That makes you unique and beautiful. At the same time, be healthy enough to where you can live to share your life with your spouse and kids. Physically fit doesn't mean looking like a particular star, but whatever is healthy and fit for you. At that point, you're your own movie star. It comes down to what you're comfortable with."

Shuges:
"Out of all, I'd have to say a movie star. Pop stars usually rely on sex appeal: tight clothes, sultry poses, etc. Too many people take their appearance more seriously than what's in their heads. Models always seem to have to be perfect. And out of the three, a movie star can get caught without makeup and it's not the end of the world. (Halle Berry in *Monster's Ball*, Charlize Theron in *Monster*. (Yes, I realize the irony of the word 'monster' in both titles.) I'd have to say a woman has gone too far when she no longer has her individuality. She's dressing like this one, acting like that one."

Slick:
"None of those! 'Do you' all of the time. Tha

Roc:
"However she feels comfortable. I know she's gone too far when I notice her makeup more than her face or conversation... or when her outfit makes me want to put on my sunglasses."

Kato:
"A woman should strive to look like anything she wants to look like. If a model, movie star, or pop star is what she desires, then by all means... go for it. If just being natural is more your cup-of-tea, then go for it. Basically, do what makes you happy about yourself. Taking it too far is being fake about it, whichever route you go."

Elliott:
"Hell no! Unless that's her profession... [then] hell yeah! [Taking it too far is] if she is superficial and programmed by mass media."

The magazines trick the women. The magazines start picking at your self-esteem. Every page you turn... you start feeling fatter and uglier, and you feel like your clothes aren't good enough. And the magazines have you forgetting how fucking beautiful you are... - Dave Chappelle, comedian and actor, from "Killin' Them Softly" (HBO)

Tahira Chloe Mahdi

Try this!

Great ways to feel attractive:

1. For one week, do not give any of your precious attention to music videos, fashion magazines, harmful television programming or any other form of entertainment that leaves you feeling like you need to change your appearance.

2. Write down all of the things about your appearance on which you've received compliments over the years. This includes all the wack lines that guys have used to get your phone number and various love notes you've received. You can buy a small notebook for under a dollar and journal them as you receive them. It's like a bank that you can go into anytime without ever running out of the treasure!

Note to Queen: Keeping the compliment does not require that you keep the person who gave it.

3. Write down all of the things you like about yourself. Do not think about anything that anybody said was wrong with you. Keep these things in your journal as well.

4. Play love songs or lustful tributes to women, sing them to yourself... and mean every word! Change any love or lust song into a LOVE YOURSELF FIRST Song.

For example:
"Foxy Lady" by Jimi Hendrix
"Loving You" by Minnie Ripperton
"Hooked On A Feeling" by Blue Swede
"Nothing Can Come Between Us" by Sade

Before you love anyone else or expect anyone to love you, you must love yourself. As your love for yourself grows, your demeanor, your appearance and life situations will reflect it. Remember, you're the Queen and others will follow your lead.

I always thought I should be treated like a star. - Madonna, singer and author

The Queendom

-your own apartment
-your own home
-a room in your parents' house
-a dorm room
-with your slob of a hunky boyfriend or husband
-a crash bed/sofa at a friend's place
-with a crazy roommate or two

  Ask yourself, "Where does Queen (Your Royal Alias) live?" What kind of place reflects the Universal power within her? Each Queen's answer will be different, but it boils down to (1) your uniqueness and (2) what you feel you deserve.

  If you decide that your current living conditions are not up to Her Majesty's standards, you can make plans to change them. However, you must constantly show appreciation and respect for your current conditions. Changing your living arrangements may take some time, so don't live in misery up until you get the place you want. Be thankful that you have a place to live and find something different about that place every day to be absolutely thrilled about.

  Look around at your belongings in your living space. As you scan each item, make a decision: Do you really *need* that? How many articles must we read about clutter and doing away with old stuff we no longer use before we give those electric blue spandex pants to some kid to use for Halloween already??

Author pauses to wipe sweat from her brow... she vows to give the purple suede skirt from senior year to the Good Will.

As the Queen, you're going to need space! Space allows you to breathe more freely. When you dance around naked to your chosen theme song, you shouldn't worry about stubbing your toe on the big box of *Seventeen* magazines kept for nostalgia's sake. That Nostalgia gal is cool, but Queen's can't consort with her too much. She's a suspected spy for *them*.

Now how about this new space you've created by letting go of unnecessary junk? It's great, right? Now you can fit in new stuff that you'll actually use – up until it becomes junk that needs to be given away or thrown out. Your social life will improve, you'll think more clearly and you will have more frequent bowel movements. See how easy that was?

Simplicity is the ultimate sophistication. - Leonardo da Vinci

The Queen Takes On... Guilt

So you've done something you're not proud of. We all have. Let it go and move on. You deserve to be happy.

DO: Pray for a lesson to be learned from what you did and how it affected those around you.

DON'T: Torture yourself by playing the situation out again and again in your mind.

DO: Pray for the courage to release the guilt.

DON'T: Feel as if you don't deserve a good life because of something you did.

DO: Be grateful that it's over.

DON'T: Waste time coming up with different endings to the situation based on what you "should" have done.

DO: Remember that you did something based on what you believed was acceptable behavior at that moment.

DON'T: Punish yourself.

DO: Be thankful that you know better than to do it again.

DON'T: Do it again.

You did it. It happened to you. Now it's over. Why are you holding on to it?

Who are you carrying the guilt for? Other people? Are you trying to show them that you have remorse? Are you carrying the guilt for yourself, feeling that you deserve punishment?

The Queen of the Universe doesn't serve herself, other people, or her Power Source by punishing herself. She serves the universe better by receiving the ever-waiting forgiveness of her Power Source. The mercy is yours for the taking. Take it, be empowered and allow yourself to do something great! Don't let guilt hold you back from Life's goodness.

Oh yes, the past can hurt. But the way I see it, you can either run from it, or... learn from it. - Rafiki, "The Lion King" (movie)

Try this!

Think of a song that best describes your past. Write down the lines and lyrics that pertain to you the most.

Examples: "Bad Girls" by Donna Summer, "Respect Yourself" by The Staple Singers

_____
_____
_____
_____
_____
_____
_____
_____

Now that you've gotten all that down, let it go! Who gives a rat's crap about your past? You're Queen of the Universe now and thinking about that past stuff is taking too much energy. Enjoy this moment. RIGHT NOW. How would you like to be feeling now? You have a choice: (1) Feel bad about your past or (2) Rejoice in your newfound power and think of something great that the Queen of the Universe would do.

So you've slept with 152 people. 89? 53? 24? 2? None?

So you've done every drug known to mankind. Only three? Just one?

So you've got a criminal record that rivals the length of this book? Just a short rap sheet? Only one time in the back of a squad car?

So you've had 4 abortions? 3? 1?

These are the biggest things that we as women tend to feel ashamed of. We can't seem to forgive ourselves for something that God has already forgiven us for. We hold on to these hard lessons learned and live lives of shame and regret.

You are NOW claiming Queen of the Universe status and that's what counts. All we have is today, yesterday is gone and we aren't even promised tomorrow. You waxed away your past indiscretions in the Royal Salon. What will you do today?

QUEEN'S RULE: I LET GO OF YESTERDAY'S PAIN TO MAKE ROOM FOR TODAY'S JOY.

I guess it comes down to a simple choice, really. Get busy livin'... or get busy dyin'. - Andy Dufresne, "The Shawshank Redemption" (movie)

What you need to give yourself before expecting it from someone else:

Love

Friendship

Forgiveness

Hope

Compliments

Confidence

Loyalty

Spirituality

Orgasms

Completion

The thing women have got to learn is that nobody gives you power; you just take it. – Roseanne Barr, comedienne and actress

Her Grace

Share the Wealth

Question: What is the difference between confidence and arrogance?

"Confidence: doesn't need to show off. Arrogance: constantly shows off." - *The Anonymous Artist*

"A confident person is one who doesn't have to brag about what she has done. Her work speaks for her character. Whenever a confident person does something, she never doubts it. She already knows that her work is good, but she does not have to broadcast it to the world. An arrogant person is always trying to seek accolades and is always bragging about what she has done. If she does not get praise for her work, then she will often times start doubting herself. Arrogance is fed by praises from other people... confidence is within the individual." - *Kenyetta*

"A confident person does not feel the need to be aggressive. An arrogant person usually forces his will or beliefs on other persons and is combative." - *Rebecca*

"Confidence is walking into a room knowing that you are a Queen. Arrogance is coming in like a tramp, looking for trouble and trying to make people feel lower than you. A confident woman makes others feel good about themselves because she feels good about herself." - *Lola*

"Confidence is knowing that you don't have to prove yourself. Arrogance is always feeling the need to prove (or should I say fool) yourself." – *SasseeDiva*

"Confidence comes from faith in a Higher Power, knowing that you are safe and doing your best. Arrogance comes from relying too much on your ego, attempting to hide your insecurity and trying to outdo others. Confidence allows you to have fun in life and be happy, while arrogance is misery because you're always feeling like you're in competition with people." –*Tahira*

"Confidence is self-preservation. Arrogance is self-modulation and it's never enough. Would you rather be coming… or going?" – *Michelle*

"Confidence is good self-esteem. Arrogance is an inferiority complex where a person looks down his/her nose at others in order to feel superior." – *Sunshine*

"Confidence is being able to accept being wrong. Arrogance is never admitting that you are wrong." – *Felicia*

Being Queen

It doesn't mean:

Being rude to people. No matter what you do for a living, show respect for the other hard working people who hold many different positions.

Being impatient and intolerant. Royalty exudes grace and patience. You're the Queen of the Universe. You always get what is best for you, anyway. Being impatient and rude is a sign of weakness. The Queen has immeasurable strength and others feel it when she walks into a room. They love it; they are attracted to it. When you do it properly, you don't even have to open your mouth.

Being an attention whore. Only babies kick and scream for attention and throw tantrums when they don't get it. A Queen is above such pettiness. There is no need to seek attention and spend your moments trying to put yourself in an imaginary spotlight. Respect and love is what a Queen gets – not because she does anything to get it, but because people believe that she deserves it.

How many times have we Queens found the strong, silent and secure type of man to be sexy? Being strong, silent and secure comes off as sexy in Queens as well. Learn it. Live it.

You must be willing to give total unconditional love to everyone, under all circumstances. That means being willing to be totally responsible for what you do and how you do it. -Iyanla Vanzant, author, inspirational speaker

Know the Difference...

Between being Queen of the Universe and being a conceited witch who thinks she's better than everyone.

Conceited Witch: snob
Queen of the Universe: selective and wise

Conceited Witch: arrogant
Queen of the Universe: confident

Conceited Witch: gold-digger
Queen of the Universe: goal-accomplisher

Conceited Witch: money taker
Queen of the Universe: money maker

Conceited Witch: thinks that only witches get respect
Queen of the Universe: is at one with Divine Love and knows that it is the most powerful force in the Universe

Conceited Witch: Isn't tolerant of others' religious/spiritual beliefs
Queen of the Universe: Accepts people as individuals while letting her Life reflect why her beliefs work for her

Conceited Witch: plays hard to get
Queen of the Universe: is hard to get (she has standards, dammit!)

I still have my feet on the ground; I just wear better shoes.
– Oprah Winfrey

KINGS SPEAK

Question: What is the difference between a confident woman and an arrogant one?

Kevin:
"A confident woman has goals, is on the move and she would love to have company on her journey. An arrogant woman can have those same positive qualities, but she wants every man to know that she does not need him. In doing so, I think she might make her man feel like she doesn't even want him."

Ben:
"I think that a confident woman is great, understands and respects her own abilities and attributes. An arrogant woman on the other hand thinks that her abilities and attributes allow the world to revolve around her."

Kato:
"A confident woman doesn't have to say anything about the qualities she possesses. They glow and she shows them in her actions. And she definitely doesn't try to show it by talking about or downgrading others. On the other hand, an arrogant woman is the total opposite. She seems to always have to talk about just how sharp she is... and one of the ways of doing that is by putting others down in the process."

Eben:
"Any woman self-proclaiming, 'I'm an independent woman,' typically is arrogant and is over compensating for some character flaw. Confident women usually are those who just do their thing without the boastfulness of the previously mentioned."

Patrick:
"A confident woman trusts herself and is capable of acting as an equal in romantic, social, or professional settings. She can behave in ways that validate her needs, but does not take actions to validate her own sense of self-worth. An arrogant woman thinks that she is better than others. She tries to validate herself by taking actions and engaging in behavior that attempts to prove this to others."

Shuges:
"A confident woman will let you win every so often because she has the confidence to know she'll get you in the next argument/disagreement. An arrogant woman isn't so sure... she'll argue to the death because she's afraid of losing any sort of assertion of power. So I guess the word (or the difference between confident and arrogant) would be insecurity."

Greg:
"A confident woman is proud of herself and who she is. She knows who she is and understands her wants and desires. What also makes her confident is that she understands the people around her (her community) and she's willing to make people around her better as a group. An arrogant woman is selfish. She is not comfortable with who she is on the inside but on the outside wants to show people that [she is] 'all of it'. She puts people down to make herself feel better. She's full of self."

Roc:
"Arrogant: 'I got my own sh*t!' This does NOT need to be communicated orally or with body language. It should radiate from her without her having to express it in any way. Women have a tendency to bring up this fact during arguments or when they feel threatened. This is absolute-

ly the last situation where a man wants/needs to hear it, especially if he's not Donald Trump. If she's not asking for anything, he'll eventually realize it anyway. Also, chicks who find it necessary to discuss their white collar jobs (or the fact that they have one) are turnoffs. Leave the job at the job. If he wants to know, he'll ask. Then, change the subject. Arrogant chicks tend to have power/control issues. I can spot these a mile away. If she feels it necessary to dominate the conversation - RUN!!!!"

Michael James:
"Confident women listen and are open-minded. They take suggestions and look toward bettering themselves mentally. Arrogant women (not to say arrogant is always a bad thing) really are not hearing what is being said and their minds are already made up."

Big:
"Confidence is courage. Courage is going into problems not knowing the outcome but believing in yourself. Arrogance is a lack of substance, foolish insecurity."

Elliott:
"A confident woman doesn't have to go out of her way [to be noticed]. She's just being herself. Arrogant women go out of their way. They try to be seen. It's a lot of silliness."

A man:
"An arrogant woman has nothing but arrogance to comfort her."

Slick:
"A confident woman is cool, down-to-earth and can adapt to any situation. An arrogant woman is selfish!"

(Remaining Anonymous):

"A confident woman knows what she has and is modest and comfortable with it. An arrogant woman is one that believes the hype that has been pumped into her head and thinks that the world revolves around her without any respect for others."

Kareem:
"The difference between a confident woman and an arrogant one is that a confident one will graciously accept any compliment or criticism you give her. An arrogant one expects compliments because people have been gassing her head up since she was knee high to a duck."

Dave:
"An arrogant woman is just someone who's full of attitude and won't listen to anyone because what she says is right. Some arrogant women are very spoiled as well. A confident woman loves herself and life!"

The Queen's Social Life

There is a difference between being alone and being lonely.

The Queen knows how to fight the lonely feeling. She's the Queen and everyone wants to be in her company. She reserves the right to stay in on a Friday night, just because. Besides, being Queen of the Universe requires you to take a break from your adoring public once in a while.

The Queen treasures any and all time spent alone. See the word "alone" as "at one". You need time to be "alone" or "at one" with God, your Power Source, the Universe, Infinite Wisdom, Divine Guidance. Your time alone is simply maintenance, like going to the gas station or charging your cell phone. It's necessary if you want to make the best use of the great gifts and powers given to you.

Don't be a "git wit", be a chameleon.

A "git wit" is slang for the phrase "get with," as in a person who tries to get with any and every thing that is going on. Be the queen who can get along – confidently and naturally – in any given situation. You don't have to compromise Her Highness's dignity or self-respect. If there is anyone you don't want to deal with, then don't. Just make sure your decision isn't based on prejudice and bigotry. You will need to be as fluid as water when dealing with different people because different situations require different things from you. A wonder and privilege of life is learning through people who are different than you. Once you are open to this, you discover that there are no major differences at all.

If you give a person the power to make you happy, you inadvertently give him/her the power to make you unhappy.

You need to make yourself happy. Better yet, *allow yourself* to be happy. Enjoy your life so that other people will be drawn to you and want to enjoy life's wonders with you. Feeling short on good company? Look at yourself. Are you having fun by yourself or are you moping around? Well, who would want to be around you with that attitude? Certainly not anyone worth sharing your time or life with. Correct YOU first. Be happy because you deserve to be. Learn to enjoy what is in your life now.

Be a good friend.

Be the Queen who listens, supports, encourages and helps. However, don't be the sort of person who is constantly seeking attention, approval, and co-dependency from others. Don't abuse your friends! They are navigating life, with its tumultuous and beautiful times, and don't need you to blow your own storm their way. It's fine to consult friends for advice, but keep it to a minimum. They are your FRIENDS, not your SHRINKS. A continuous cycle of pity only leads down the road of loneliness because you're alienating anyone who allows you the pleasure of his or her friendship.

Don't be too sweet lest you be eaten up; don't be too bitter lest you be spewed out. - Jewish proverb

Mirror, Mirror

How skin problems can provide us with a sense of security

Some Queens have never quite felt as if they could be themselves. They are dying to show the world who they really are... dying to express themselves individually, but they're afraid of what others will think.

As much emphasis is placed on being "beautiful," some Queens are not comfortable with their natural "good looks". *(Please note that beauty is in the eye of the beholder. These statements are not in compliance with any fashion or entertainment standard.)* As a matter of fact, early trauma associated with a bully or jealous peers can mold a woman's entire life into hiding from her beauty. Some Queens are born with what may be considered beauty by a fashion-industry standard but their personalities don't mix well with that false sense of glamour.

Acne is common among teens because that is the time in our lives that we are most insecure with who we are. Sometimes, we don't begin to feel insecure until we reach the point where we're expected to do well for ourselves, such as college or the business world. Feeling bad or uncomfortable about any aspect of who you are can summon acne to stand guard for you.

Acne is a burden. Why would a woman hold onto something that would bring her ridicule?
People falling into these categories have a subconscious need to wear a mask. Acne is that mask. Circumstances may vary but it all boils down to a desire to hide or blend in. When we aren't comfortable with who we are or when we are afraid to show the world our

true selves, acne comes to our rescue. It makes the "beautiful" seem more ordinary and the really unique seem to blend in with everyone else. Acne is terribly annoying and people do all they can to stop it, but it serves a purpose. Or else, it wouldn't be there.

Are there any other reasons for breakouts?
Breakouts, as well as skin rashes that seems to come from allergic reactions, are a means of protection against others. When people "get under our skin," our internal discomfort may actually manifest on the outside - *under our skin*.

Sharing the Wealth:
"Whenever I find myself in a new relationship, I experience back-to-back breakouts. It seems as if I am trying to protect my feelings. The same goes for when I am trying to leave a relationship. It is astonishing how my skin can be almost TOTALLY clear... until I'm around the man I am trying to break up with. In these cases, it's almost as if my anger and resentment are rising to the surface, or once again, I am protecting myself from hurt feelings."
- Tahira

What about the foods we eat?
Excessive sugar, alcohol and caffeine can contribute to the feelings of insecurity, anxiety and paranoia we are already struggling to overcome. The more insecure and anxious we feel, the more prone we are to breakouts. Eating more vegetables and drinking more water contribute to our body's sense of general well-being. Top that off with regular exercise and stress is greatly minimized. Hence, the frequency of breakouts is reduced significantly.

What's a Queen to do?
The first step to releasing frequent breakouts is

being comfortable with who you are and what you have to offer the world. In order to release acne, a Queen must first release her concern about what other people think about her. When she no longer feels the need to hide, blend in, or protect her feelings, the acne goes away on its own.

If there are people around you who you would like to stay away from, let go of harmful attitudes toward them. They need to be released with an overwhelming feeling of love and goodwill. It helps to make positive affirmations about them when feelings of contempt arise. Also, you must make positive affirmations about yourself and your own power! You must not give power to the ill will you are imagining that people have toward you.

Protection is what we are in need of. Take a cue from Moses, the historical hero who led a great number of people to freedom while being pursued by an army. When his people became afraid at the approaching of the army and found themselves standing at a sea which they could conceive of no way to cross, Moses told them that they must not be afraid. He assured them that God would fight for them! Your Power Source is the ONLY power, the power of good. Allow this power to protect you and fight for you. The battle is not yours and you do yourself a great disservice by taking it on as your own.

QUEEN'S RULE: I RELEASE ALL FEAR. I AM GUIDED AND PROTECTED BY THE MOST HIGH GUARDIAN.

If there is no enemy inside, the enemy outside can't do anything. – African Proverb

Peace in Friendships

Consider those friends, relatives and lovers who constantly share their life's issues with you. You're not a direct part of their crazy situations and can usually provide good advice simply because you're on the outside looking in. However, think of how often these people actually *take* your advice. This is one clue that will help you separate the instances when they want your advice from the times they want you to just LISTEN.

Sometimes people just need an ear or a shoulder. They can talk themselves into a solution. There are times when we all simply need to "vent" without fear of criticism, judgment or even a voice of reason. If you are open to hearing the problems of others, be more of a good listener. Give up the need to tell them that they are wrong, unreasonable or immoral. Being a supportive friend does not mean that you condone behaviors; it means that you allow friends to learn their own lessons.

At the same time, being a good friend is putting a limit on how much stress you bring to those closest to you. You must trust your Power Source to be the Divine Guidance and Infinite Intelligence that it is. Silence is golden and a clear head can be a foundation for miraculous solutions. It is not always necessary to ask around for advice or a sympathetic ear. Learn to search yourself for answers to all that you need to know. You'll feel powerful, peaceful and smart as a whip by simply choosing a connection with your Power Source over a vent fest with a friend. (See page 53 for another alternative.)

Listen with Love. Be open to hear the messages that the Universe sends. Choose peace, not discord, in all of your relationships.

Some people without brains do an awful lot of talking.
– Scarecrow, "The Wizard of Oz" (movie)

Try this!

Are you one of the millions who have a problem with ROAD RAGE?? Here are helpful tips to cool you down the next time someone drives too slowly, cuts you off, or won't let you over in traffic.

-Instead of cursing, shout a line to one of your favorite songs. If you're listening to music, sing along loudly to whatever is on.

-Instead of calling them a nasty name, call them a nice name. Yell, "Genius!" or "Beautiful!"

-Instead of ranting about what driving faux pas they just committed, you can shout, "Thanks a lot!" or "You're a great driver!"

Of course, your tone of voice will be very angry and loud. The key here is to make yourself laugh in order to alleviate your stress. Don't you have enough to deal with? Sarcasm has helped many people with frustrating situations. Why shouldn't driving be one of them?

Don't follow closely behind them while honking the horn and flashing your lights. It does no good and these days, people might get violent. Carry yourself as if you were the Queen of the Universe.

Holding on to anger is like grasping a hot coal with the intent of throwing it at someone else; you are the one getting burned.
- Buddha, 568 - 488 BC

Oh, the Drama!

Share the Wealth

Question: What is the difference between a Queen and a drama queen?

"A Queen is above pettiness and drama but a drama queen thrives on it." – *Sunshine*

"A Queen builds her kingdom on her triumphs and successes. She empowers and inspires. A drama queen builds her kingdom on excuses and negativity. Unlike a drama queen, A Queen has so much going for herself, that she neither needs nor has time to create 'drama' to be powerful. A drama queen must create 'drama' to make herself feel important or useful." – *Dionne*

"A Queen is a woman who is confident in herself. She's secure and assertive. A drama queen needs to be loud and make sure everyone knows she's a 'queen'. A real Queen has the look and demeanor, so being loud to make her title known to everyone else is not necessary. They can tell by the way she walks and the way she speaks." – *Samantha*

"A Queen doesn't have to 'act a fool' to get attention. Her royal presence speaks for itself, whereas a drama queen has to constantly put on a show in order to get attention. If she did not put on a show, she would probably never get any attention... or at least that is what she thinks." - *Kenyetta*

"A Queen actually has power. A drama queen has the pretense of it." - *Felicia*

"A Queen is a person who takes charge of a situation and comes out victorious. A drama queen unnecessarily makes a big deal of a situation without solving the problem and while involving others in the drama. Talking about a situation and handling a situation are two different things." - *Lola*

"A drama queen demands attention; a Queen commands attention." - *Rebecca*

"A Queen knows who she is without creating drama whereas a drama queen creates drama but doesn't realize her potential of becoming a queen." - *SasseeDiva*

"A drama queen is always calling someone (a man, a friend, a family member) to help her with something or just listen to her nonstop whining about it. She can't stand not being the center of attention and she tells a lot of her personal business (even if she has to make something up). In a conversation, you can't get a word in because she's hell-bent on being the center of attention! A Queen loves solving her own problems and relies on strong spiritual beliefs or her own persevering nature (instead of the sympathy of others) to make it through. She is loving, humble and levelheaded. She walks tall in God's glory, not because she thinks she looks good." - *Tahira*

Queen of the Universe vs. The Drama Queen

Queens of the Universe don't demand attention using immature demonstrations. They receive respect because of the way they carry themselves.

On the other hand, a drama queen craves attention and will do anything to get it.

Alias: The Attention Whore

Known to:
-destroy property
-fake tearful breakdowns
-have lots of real tearful breakdowns
-start arguments
-start and spread rumors
-tell lies (small and totally outrageous)
-talk way too much

She doesn't care whether the attention is positive or negative and most likely can't tell the difference after years of this immature behavior.

She's always in some kind of crisis, trying to pull everyone around her into it. She may appear popular because of her looks, her money, her clothes, or something else that can easily be taken away from her. In actuality, no one likes her. She's horribly annoying and she drains and alienates everyone she comes into contact with.

In relationships, she is very demanding. She wants a man's constant attention and will use sex, crying, yelling and stalking in order to obtain it. Her actions ruin her serious relationships, but in seeking any and all attention, she is the ultimate rebounder.

A drama queen doesn't have self-control. She's lost it somewhere along the way in her quest for attention. Too busy trying to manipulate the emotions of others, she has sent her own emotions on a roller coaster crash course.

The Brat In the Sandbox

Interestingly enough, a drama queen is usually very attractive, well dressed, and enjoying her job or career. Women who don't know her very well might envy the drama queen. On the outside, she's the woman who has it all. Those closest to the drama queen may envy her material possessions, looks, or the attention she receives, but they don't envy her as a person. They have seen her inside and out and they know it gets really ugly underneath the surface.

In their quest for attention, drama queens frequently call their friends and family with dramatic nonsense about everything under the sun. Though they constantly seek and receive help and advice, they have no plans to actually solve a problem. It is attention, sympathy and a false sense of validation that they seek. If a drama queen's friends called her for that same emotional support, sympathetic ear, or trust, she wouldn't be able to provide it. Instead, she would change the conversation to talk about her own problems, cut the conversation short out of dissatisfaction with not being the center of attention, or not listen at all because she really doesn't care about the problems of her friends. When she can, she will absorb enough information to use against others and to make herself appear superior in some way.

These women are addicted to the drama of unhealthy relationships and situations because of the attention they receive when they attempt to share the chaos with others. Friends and family wonder why they stay in bad relationships or bounce from one disaster to another. The answer is simple. Dramatic situations provide a great way for them to remain the center of attention – even if it's negative.

Just as sure as misery loves company, drama queens love to drag others into their pit of unhappiness. They subconsciously create bad situations such as car trouble, illness, injury, fights, and anything that would require someone to come to their aid. As often as possible, they test the loyalty and reliability of those closest to them because they are so insecure with themselves. Drama queens don't realize that they drive everyone away from them. Instead, they feel as if the world owes them lots of attention and they will do almost anything to get it.

Drama queens usually feel as if their friends and family aren't there for them. They can't see the fact that they have simply overused people's comforting shoulders, quality time, listening ears, precious trust, and sometimes, their hard-earned money. A drama queen believes that other women are jealous of her (and some may be) but this won't stop her from trying to get their attention and attempting to outshine them whenever possible.

A drama queen often changes "friends". She has a false sense of loyalty to "friends" as long as they are able to withstand her drama. Once the "friends" get wise to her game, they disappear and the drama queen moves

...ext "friends" who will give her an audience for her life's messes. A drama queen also often hangs out with people whom she doesn't like. Her goal in doing this is to ensure herself an audience or a few people that she can outshine. She will go back and forth to old "friends" as often as they let her. Again, she is satisfied as long as she has an audience or someone to manipulate.

People can cry much easier than they can change. - James Baldwin, novelist and essayist

Set Her Free

A drama queen is quick to guilt trip those around her. Don't fall into her traps! She is a master at manipulation. You are NOT obligated to be there for her every hissy fit. A Queen of the Universe deserves to be happy. If you have a friend who is a drama queen, deal with her when you can handle it mentally. It is essential to pick and choose when you are comfortable with listening to your friends' problems. Why should you have to keep coming to the drama queen's rescue and listening to her whining when what she really needs is a good therapist?

If you are open to listening to the problems of your friends, relatives and lovers, try not to take these problems on as your own. Instead, keep them in your prayers and wish them all the best in working the situation out for themselves. Taking on too many problems of others can affect your health. The most common symptoms that show you are shouldering too many burdens of others are: acne on your back, pain in your shoulders, and problems with your breasts and ears.

If someone has a problem that is simple enough

for you to help with (comfortably), then do a good deed and be done with it. Be careful not to allow yourself to be used or manipulated.

Getting Help for the Drama Queen

If you fit the description of a drama queen and are honest enough with yourself to know it...

There is nothing wrong with seeing a therapist. Your friends and family are neither qualified nor properly emotionally equipped to deal with your life's issues. Stop stressing them out with your problems. Check your local listings for crisis lines and other sources of help – professional help. There are people who have made it their life's work to talk to people who need emotional stability. Let your friends be your friends. They don't get paid enough to put up with your drama.

Do not self-medicate with drugs. Prescribed drugs are just as harmful and addictive as illegal ones. The only difference is the government gets money (legally) from the prescribed ones. Drugs can make you even more of a hazard to those around you.

Prioritize. Do you need to be in a relationship right now? Dragging some poor, unsuspecting guy down into the pit of your drama will only worsen your misery later on in the relationship. If he's smart, he'll run screaming in the other direction when he wises up to your antics and you'll be alone again. Love yourself first. Help yourself first. Be at your best when going into a relationship so that you can demand the best in a partner.

As far as friendships go, learn how to be your own friend first. Can you stand to be alone with yourself?

Could you handle a whole weekend, for example, all by yourself without talking to another person (email included)? If the thought of not talking to or communicating with another person (not including your kids) for a few days makes you uneasy... then you are not giving yourself the chance to get to know the real you. Maybe you know the real you and you don't like yourself. That is nothing to be ashamed of or to take out on other people. Those bad feelings toward yourself can be changed. You may want to stock up on self-help and inspirational books to get started on the path to self-love. But most of all, you need your POWER SOURCE!

Insanity: doing the same thing over and over again and expecting different results. - Albert Einstein

KINGS SPEAK

Question: What is the difference between a Queen and a drama queen?

Big:
"I got one word for you: overreaction! The rule of a Queen is that the Queen rules the place. A drama queen only thinks she does."

Patrick:
"A Queen is someone who gains attention from others by giving her time, attention, love, and affection. She can be pretty or plain, but her attention is earned through her attentiveness. A drama queen needs attention and gains it by creating or sustaining events that force her into a limelight. Whether by evoking sympathy, support, sexual attention, or anger, a drama queen takes attention from others by thrusting herself into situations that demand attention from others without giving anything of herself in return."

A man:
"Drama queens are starving for attention and are needy. Queens draw attention without trying. They can be themselves and are beautiful inside and out. Queens are the keepers. Drama queens get dumped."

Roc:
"Drama queen: insecure; chicks who feel it necessary to do loud arguing; disrespectful chicks; chicks who get physical during an argument (or who throw things); constantly bringing up [a man's] ex because she keeps wondering; chicks who can't act professionally in public; tire slashers/revenge chicks. If she turns off the television

when I'm watching it, that's a red flag.

"Chicks who constantly need to be in control also get the red flag. If she's in (or ever was in) therapy, she may fall into this category. Watch out. If we argue more than once a week, she's a drama queen. I know I'm not into drama and I'm easy to get along with, so it must be her.

"Queen: secure; politely brushes you off. *Why don't you go to the strip club? Here's a few dollars.* Professional, cool, collected. *Honey I have a problem -let's talk.*"

(Remaining Anonymous):
"A Queen is a woman that has herself together and is worthy of respect and admiration. A drama queen is one that causes drama or is full of drama because she wants the respect and admiration a Queen [receives], but doesn't know how to go about getting it and shows it by showing her ass."

Kareem:
"The difference between a Queen and a drama queen is that most Queens I know are drama free and intend on staying that way. Drama queens' lives are more complicated than any people I know."

Shuges:
"Humility. A Queen doesn't mind another woman trying to be like her. A drama queen acts as if all the attention MUST be on her as well as the fact that no other woman can or should be like her. Drama queens act as if they're the only ones that can set a trend, come up with a brilliant idea, or make a significant difference/impact with whatever they're involved in."

Elliott:
"A Queen is at peace with herself and her environment.

She understands that everything is in Divine Order and handles challenges without the drama. A drama queen is the direct opposite."

Michael James:
"A Queen is someone you adore, respect and want to give the world to. A drama queen is one you really don't want to be around."

Dave:
"A drama queen thinks that she's all that! Loves attention, and no one can tell her anything because she's the shhh...[sic] However, drama queens attract more negative critics from friends, family, and possibly people who don't know her."

Greg:
"It goes back to the confident woman and the arrogant one. A queen is that confident woman, that leader, that mother, that counselor, that friend who will make others around her better. She is comfortable with who she is.

"A drama queen... attention always has to be on

her. Like the arrogant woman, she is not confident in who she is. Because she's not comfortable with who she is, she wants to bring attention to herself with bright red hair, fishnet pantyhose, really short skirts. She's bringing attention, [she is] psychotic, crazy, has a whole bunch of issues, but she's fine than a mutha!"

Mark:
"The Queen knows that drama is not something she needs to bring to her man to gain attention, but a drama queen will do everything possible to bring on this conflict. They need this negative energy to feel wanted or loved."

Kevin:
"A Queen knows what she wants out of a relationship and recognizes whether she can find that in a man. If so, she may pursue something serious. If not, she moves on. A drama queen asks why can't she find what she's looking for, and tries to whine, cry, curse and drama (yeah, I invented a new verb) what she wants out of the wrong dude... over and over and over and over again."

Try This!

You know that friend you have who seems to understand all the crap you go through? Whether it's your childhood issues or on-the-job headaches, this person will listen to your every woe and even swap life's horror stories with you over drinks and dessert.

The next time you feel yourself getting into a "woe is us" venting session with this friend, switch gears!

Have an "All Hail the Queen" jamboree instead! Talk about what's great in your life, how you've overcome some BS and why you're so thankful. Literally count your blessings down to what seems to be the most insignificant. Having something to complain about is a crutch that you can throw away NOW! Stand tall and rejoice!

Look at where you are in Life! Congratulations, Queen! You've made it through some rough times! It's a miracle you're still here!

Now, there. Don't you just feel like the Queen of the Universe?

I want to walk through life instead of being dragged through it.
- Alanis Morissette, singer

Her Majesty

Share the Wealth

Request: Name a song, book or movie that made you feel empowered as a woman.

Dionne's inspiration:
Movie: "9 to 5" – The actresses in that movie showed the world that women can be more than secretaries and assistants; women can successfully lead, manage, and operate companies. It helped women venture to break the glass ceiling in corporate America.
Movie: "Places in the Heart" – In spite of the odds stacked against her, Sally Field's character - a widow with two children during the depression - did what she had to do to keep her family together. From taking in a blind border to hiring an ex-slave to lead her laborers, Field's character had a will and drive to survive. That took strength, courage, and tenacity.

Michelle's inspiration:
The song "Seventeen" by Janis Ian shows that all types of women need love. I realized that I was a real person and deserved love and respect.

Terria's inspiration:
Chaka Khan's "I'm Every Woman" made me feel empowered as a woman because "I'm every woman, It's

all in me..." This song just inspired me to do anything and be anything that I hoped to. For instance, I could walk into a job interview and display confidence and enjoy the company of girlfriends and the single life. Not forgetting the fast tempo of the song...it made me want to dance and sing (okay, okay...try to sing or at least hum the words). I was celebrating me, myself, and I... funny, serious, extraordinary, wonderful and beautiful. Sing on Chaka...sing on.

Samantha's inspiration:
"Prime of my Life" by Phyllis Hyman. This song is for young women who can do anything they put their mind to. She sings, "I'm in the prime of my life, growing stronger everyday – moving mountains standing in my way." How powerful is that?!

Tahira's inspiration:
"Free" by Deniece Williams. I silently sing that to myself when I meet a man I'm interested in. He has to understand that I want to be free and I've got to be me. As the lyrics state: "Let's not waste ecstasy, 'cause I'll only be here for a while." I don't want, nor will I give, a lot of arguing.
I am energized by watching "Fried Green Tomatoes" and "Steel Magnolias" because they showed how women could inspire each other to find strength and overcome difficulties. Women need to do more to uplift other women instead of judging them by their status, looks, past, or choice of profession (i.e. prostitution and exotic dancing).

Sunshine's inspiration:
"The Color Purple". The women overcame oppression from spouses and family members who had no idea how to love them.

Lola's inspiration:
    The movie "Beaches". Two friends from different walks of life supported each other in times of need. Also, any song by Al Green!

Terri's inspiration:
    Gloria Gaynor's song "I Will Survive".

Rebecca's inspiration:
    The song "I'm Every Woman".

SasseeDiva's inspiration:
    My #1 women's empowerment song is Mary J. Blige's "No More Drama"!

The Queen Takes On... Loneliness

The next time you have time to yourself – a few hours, a whole day or most of a week – learn to treasure the privacy and shelter of the situation.

DO: Take this time to get to know and love yourself more. No matter how much you think you already do, there is always room for more Love.

DON'T: Wallow in misery or think self-destructive thoughts.

DO: Go through old photo albums and let good memories keep you company.

DON'T: Dwell on any bad memories that could make you feel lonely AND angry. Be careful not to play a comparison game with your past and your present. All you have is NOW... make the best of it!

DO: Get out a recipe book and make something tasty.

DON'T: Snack on foods that are harmful. You know which ones they are; stop making excuses.

DO: Watch a good movie or read a book.

DON'T: Feel like you absolutely need to leave the house or be around other people.

DO: Put effort into a home project or your dream career.

DON'T: Call a person who will try to make you feel bad for not calling more often. (And they wonder why people don't call them.) Queens don't do guilt trips.

DO: Call an elderly relative who would love to hear from you or a friend you haven't spoken to in a few months.

DON'T: Call people and try to make them feel guilty about YOUR loneliness. It's YOUR issue, not theirs.

Take this time to get to know and love YOU. If you can't stand to be alone with yourself, what makes you think anyone else wants to be around you? Once you get used to enjoying your own company, others will follow your lead.

Other things to do when you're alone:
-Play one of your "Queen of the Universe" CDs and dance to it while singing. (See page 209.)

-Attempt to make a very intimate connection with your Power Source. You can use methods of meditation, many of which can be found in books, videos and on the World Wide Web.

Spending time to enjoy the naturally peaceful moments in your life is a privilege that only a few are wise enough to take advantage of. A person who treasures peace also finds that they are more receptive to Divine Wisdom – the One Mind of Infinite Knowledge that can bring us all the answers we need if we just listen. If you are using all of your free time to watch television, read magazines, and talk to friends, your mind is constantly being overwrought with other people's thoughts and ideas. The Queen of the Universe can think for herself and she chooses Divine Guidance.

If you're feeling lonely once a week or more, seek help. This problem does not have to haunt you for the rest of your life. You can change your attitude, determine the root of the problem and live a Life filled with Love.

QUEEN'S RULE: I AM NEVER LONELY BECAUSE I AM CONNECTED TO AN IMMEASURABLE FORCE OF LOVE AND POWER.

If I am searching for my spirituality, passionately, I must begin with me. There's just me. One is the magic number. – Jill Scott, "One Is The Magic #" (song)

Choosing Victory over Sympathy

Maybe we didn't get the sympathy we needed at the time of a tragedy in our lives such as abuse, rape, an abortion, loss of a job or the loss of someone we loved. Due to feelings of emptiness and resentment, many people continuously create bad situations in their lives in attempts to get sympathy or because they don't know how to live with anything other than pain.

Don't seek sympathy... seek victory! After all you've been through, don't you deserve it?

You should feel good about how far you've come. It is not necessary to keep yourself buried in pain. Forgive and forget. A good measure of success is how you feel about people who've wronged you in the past. If you really feel that you are doing well in life, there is no need to harbor resentment. Look at it this way... did they really keep you from achieving your goals?

Claim your victory over your past, over those hurts, over those people. Choose to be healthy and free. When we seek sympathy or make a habit of feeling sorry for ourselves, different illnesses and diseases take over our bodies. We subconsciously let our natural defenses down and allow ourselves to become ill, and that's how we get sympathy - even from ourselves - when all else fails.

If you sincerely believe that someone stopped you from accomplishing something important, use that as motivation to move on. If you wallow in self-pity and blame, thinking about what could have been, then you are giving others the power to erase your dreams. Why would you give anyone that power? Make new goals for yourself and put positive energy into accomplishing them.

The best revenge is success. If they were trying to destroy you, wouldn't it just eat them up inside to see you doing well? Don't let them win. This is YOUR life. Enjoy it.

Enjoy yourself. It's later than you think. – Chinese Proverb

The Ex-Factor

When an acquaintance or meddling, well-meaning family member says, "What ever happened to (ex who hurt you)?" respond by asking, "Who?"

Forgive him and forget him. You have successfully released the pain of that past relationship when you are able to wish the ex nothing but happiness.

You can forgive and forget that person, but remember the lesson you learned. Everything from Your Power Source is a blessing. Be happy because that hurtful person is no longer in your life causing you pain. We are advised to "forget" because the memories of what these people did to us can cause us pain whenever we think about them.

Knock that chip off your shoulder! It totally does NOT go with your outfit! You're so busy shouldering that miserable burden, you'll be too irritated to notice Mr. Right For You (or all the honeys you can date in the meantime).

Not the cry, but the flight of the wild duck, leads the flock to fly and follow. – Chinese Proverb

WORDPLAY
I say, *"No way"* to that cliché.

These sayings didn't come from wisdom and a healthy attitude toward life. They came from bitterness and a victim's mentality. Queens of the Universe are not victims; they're victors! Erase the following sentiments from your consciousness:

"Love hurts."
Many people go through tons of unnecessary crap in relationships, believing that love is supposed to hurt. Put a person in their lives who would treat them well and they'd find any excuse not to be loved the way that love was meant to be. They will never attract a healthy, happy relationship, simply because they have internalized a belief that love hurts. Tell yourself the truth: do you get off on drama and discord or do you really want a healthy, loving relationship?

"Money doesn't grow on trees."
Have you ever wondered why some people have so much money (even the celebrities with zero talent) and others have so little (even the talented, hardworking ones)? People with money feel as if they *deserve* it. Whether they "worked hard" for it or were born into it, they think of money as something positive and possible for them. Do you think you deserve to have an abundance of money?

"I'll be happy when..."
People who say this are never happy. They may have a few happy occasions, but the feeling dies quickly. You don't have until 'when'. All you have is now. The next five minutes aren't promised; neither are the possessions you're failing to be thankful for. Things could always be

worse. Don't talk yourself into a *really* bad situation. Are you willing to accept yourself for where you are in your life at this moment?

"Whatever can go wrong, will."
(also known as Murphy's Law)
Why in the universe anyone would want to spend treasured moments embracing this thought is a mystery. In the book *The Game of Life and How to Play It*, author Florence Scovel Shinn writes, "If one asks for success and prepares for failure, he will get the situation he has prepared for." Expect the worst and you will run into it very often. Trust your Power Source and begin to see the doors that open when one closes. Re-think the way you are examining your life's situations. Are you willing to let your mind and heart see the silver lining when your eyes only see the clouds?

QUEEN'S RULE: MY WORDS CARRY FABULOUS POWER AND THEY RESONATE THROUGHOUT MY EMPIRE, THE UNIVERSE. I CHOOSE MY WORDS WITH LOVE ONLY.

Loyalty to a petrified opinion never yet broke a chain or freed a human soul. - Mark Twain, author

Whatcha Really Want

"Be careful what you wish for because you just might get it." How many times have you wanted something - a particular job, a particular love interest, *anything* - and was so disappointed in the result, you dreaded the day you ever wished for it?

Don't accept other people's ideas of what you *should* want and don't stress yourself out until you get what you want. Part of getting what you want is appreciating what you already have.

If you don't know what you want, don't despair. That's what your Power Source is there for. Submit to the will of your Power Source. Tell your Power Source, "Let thy will be done." There are ways of bringing you Life's best that you aren't even aware of. Why try to squeeze mediocre solutions out of your puny human capabilities when your Power Source is available to take charge and use a power greater than anything you can conceive of? Invite miracles! You're not in this alone!

Losing It

Have you lost or misplaced something? No need to worry or drive yourself nuts looking for it. You can never lose anything that was meant for you to keep.

In your state of grace as Queen of the Universe, you find comfort in knowing that some things have to be removed from your life in order to make room for something better. This includes a material possession or a personal relationship (friend or lover). We lose things in order to learn lessons about our lives. Each Queen has her own lessons to learn and each experience of losing something carries its own message.

"Everything has a season." Some things are meant to only be in your life for a certain period of time. Those things may be appropriate for one stage in your life but not in another. For example: You are now reaching a higher level of consciousness and awareness. Various friends, lovers, habits and negative beliefs will not be conducive to what you need to continue your ascent to peace and high self-esteem. Along with your newfound path, you will find yourself facing new people, things, and thoughts that mirror your happiness.

The wise man in the storm prays to God, not for safety from danger, but for deliverance from fear. – Ralph Waldo Emerson, poet and essayist

The Queen Takes On... The Critics

DO: Improve your self-esteem and sense of self-worth so that you only attract people who give you loving advice, not criticism.

DON'T: Get used to being around a bunch of critical people. You don't have to embrace criticism if you don't want to.

DO: Remember that opinions are like a—holes. Everybody's got one.

DON'T: Accept everything a critic says as the truth.

DO: Treat others as you would like to be treated. Accept them as they are and people will do the same for you.

DON'T: Criticize others, even celebrities and total strangers. You're doing it to make yourself feel better, but it doesn't do anything but keep you in a state of bitterness and bring more criticism your way.

DO: Notice that most people criticize others because of their own personal insecurities.

DON'T: Lash back at critics too much or too harshly. The Queen is graceful and she can let her work and deeds say it all.

DO: Keep your determination and faith. The best revenge is always success!

DON'T: Let them see you sweat. That's what gives them satisfaction.

Sometimes, we feel criticized only because we haven't received accolades and public praise for our work, art, or accomplishments. That's no way to live. Don't look outside of yourself for approval. Be thankful and appreciative of your own talents, passions, hobbies, lessons learned and unique qualities. Revel in them and don't take them for granted.

Remember, you are supposed to be doing the work of your Power Source and letting that Divine force guide your steps in whatever projects you undertake. Find your peace and motivation in this and this only. Why accept discouragement from people who are obviously just as scared as you are?

I'll never let a statue tell me how nice I am. - A Tribe Called Quest, "Award Tour" (song)

I find that the very things that I get criticized for, which is usually being different and just doing my own thing and just being original, is the very thing that's making me successful.
- Shania Twain, singer

Try this!

If you feel hurt or wronged in any way by someone who was once close to you, forgiveness may be the last thing on your mind. Here are a few steps that may help you deal with your anger.

-Ask God to help you forgive this person. It's difficult to forget what the person did to you but ask Your Power Source to help you release the resentment from your consciousness. It's just a burden anyway and is another source of stress.

-Really make an effort to forgive and release. When that person crosses your mind, tell yourself, "I wish him/her well," or "I give him/her to my Power Source."

-Send that person a friendly greeting card or leave a nice message on their answering machine when you know they won't be home. Don't include the phrase, "I forgive you."

-Forget the nice gesture and move on with your wonderful life as Queen of the Universe.

A simple act of forgiving and forgetting can guarantee at least one miracle soon after. However, your goal must be to release the pain that person has caused you – not just to get a reward. Think of the act as you rewarding yourself by letting go of the burden of resentment.

QUEEN'S RULE: WHAT GOES AROUND COMES AROUND. I WISH OTHERS WELL.

Share the Wealth

Question: What is the best advice your mother ever gave you?

"Girl, stop being so damned mean." - *SasseeDiva*

"Never get involved with a man who has more problems than you!" - *Rebecca*

"Learn how to be independent," "Learn how to drive," and "Learn how to take care of a family." - *Lola*

"Remember, you reap what you sow." - *Samantha*

"Follow your heart." - *Terri*

"Don't depend on anyone, especially a man, to take care of you," "Get a good education," and "Don't marry a drunk." - *Sunshine*

"To finish what I start - to have a finishing spirit and see all of my projects through, because that is what many people who are rich today do. They finish what they start, no matter what the outcome is." - *Kenyetta*

"When you leave a room, look behind you; make sure you didn't leave anything. How profound that turned out to be. (Actually, anything OUT OF PLACE.)" - *Michelle*

"What goes on at home stays at home!" - *Dionne*

"You may think he's cute now but before you have sex with him, imagine what a little one of him would look like," "Don't get mad when your period comes unexpectedly. Would you rather be inconvenienced for a short time or for the next few years?" and "Don't cry for any man who isn't crying for you!"- *Tahira*

"Better to be alone than in bad company." - *Felicia*

"With honey, you catch a lot more flies than with vinegar." - *The Anonymous artist*

The Queen Takes On...
The Overbearing Family

DO: Remember, your parents were once like you and *their* parents started this crap. Channel anger into sympathy for them.

DON'T: Hate them. It's a horrible burden.

DO: Let your attitude and actions show your family how great you're doing.

DON'T: Try to make them feel sorry for you. You're the Queen, you don't need sympathy!

DO: When they start in on you, repeat your positive affirmations. OUT LOUD.

DON'T: Engage them in meaningless debates about your life.

DO: Turn every family gathering into a party so you can have just enough alcohol to deal with them.*

DON'T: Get sloppy drunk just before you see them.

DO: Accept yourself and your uniqueness. Make them want to be like you!

DON'T: Try to be like them. You have to make your own path.

*This won't work if you see them more than once every few weeks. You'll end up being the crazy drunk in the family and Queens don't need the added burden of alcoholism.

If you cannot get rid of the family skeleton, you may as well make it dance. - George Bernard Shaw, playwright, author, journalist

Try this!

Do a "180" for a day! Pick a day when you have the time and the attitude to flip your personality. This is the most fun when played with a group of Queens out and about on the town.

If you're the Queen who's usually burdened with the role of "Ms. Responsible"... Do something wild! Knock the socks off of everyone you're scared of disappointing. They'll most likely respect you more for your show of fearlessness. Note: This does not include such extremes as getting arrested (unless it's for a cool protest) or neglecting your kids (at least get a sitter).

If you're the Queen who's always accused of being a little too rambunctious... Play the shy, mysterious role this time! Shock the finger-pointers and attract fresh inquisitors who will be intensely intrigued.

Your "180" may call for experimentation with wigs, makeup, bars, people, unfamiliar shoes and/or underwear. Hey, actors often need props. Just remember that it is safe to go back to the real you. Have fun!

Queen Theme: "Man! I Feel Like A Woman!" by Shania Twain

With hair, heels and attitude, honey, I am through the roof.
- RuPaul, singer

Share the Wealth

Request: Name an old school tradition that should be brought back to save current and future generations.

"An old school trick that should still be enforced is for our little-women-to-be to keep a dime between their knees, and for our little men to be real men by taking care of [their] responsibilities." – *SasseeDiva*

"Having family time/dinner/games; family outings!" – *Rebecca*

"Afros... everybody should have them. Life was good when they were in style. Men spent more time in the mirror and less in the street. And that includes all ethnicities." - *Michelle*

"Family reunions; giving the children their fathers' last names; eating dinner together as a family at least once a week." – *Sunshine*

"Other people/neighbors looking out for your kids." - *Lola*

"Family Dinners. They are a great opportunity for a family to regroup, bond, and communicate. This tradition emphasized that family is a priority, and reminded us that our families can serve as a source of strength. Ok, this isn't quite 'old school,' but it is something that is not common in most families." – *Dionne*

"Going to [place of worship] as a family. I think too many of us don't do that nowadays." – *Terri*

"Block parties." – *Felicia*

"Knowing how and when to play the good girl role like the ladies in the classic movies. Now, *they* knew how to seduce a man with class! Also, getting to know someone before making the decision to have sex. That would eliminate all the wishes for 'take-backs'." - *Tahira*

"Teachers that are empowered to do their jobs."
– *Anonymous artist*

Her Excellency

Your Current Job vs. Your Dream Job

Put a check beside the statement that best defines your current job or career.

__ It's the one I've dreamed of since the 4th grade "What I Want to Be When I Grow Up" essay and I love it!

__ It's what I thought I really wanted to do but I'm here and it sucks.

__ It's the one I've planned since the high school "Career Day" and I love it!

__ I've never known what I wanted to do and yes, my job sucks.

__ It's the one I've wanted since the 1st, 2nd or 3rd time I switched my college major and I love it!

__ It's nothing like what I've always pictured for myself and it sucks.

__ It's nothing like what I've always pictured myself doing, but I love it anyway.

__ It's a cool job, but I know it is not my true calling. I am not fulfilled.

Your Majesty, you've heard this before, but maybe you'll actually believe it this time. It is never too late or too early to follow your dreams. Some queens have a clear, defined picture of their career goals, others have a very close idea, and some have absolutely no clue. Whatever your situation, it is imperative that you are happy with your means of income. You may even find yourself with two jobs for a while - the one that sucks can provide funds for pursuing what you really want to do.

I used to want the words "She tried" on my tombstone. Now I want, "She did it." - Katherine Dunham, dancer and choreographer

Your Career and Your Power Source

As Queen of the Universe, you will become an expert at prayer, meditation, and directly communicating with your Power Source in order to be guided to what is best for you. Finding a great-paying, spiritually fulfilling job for yourself is another perfect reason to make that intimate connection. If you allow, your Power Source can lead you to the job that is right for you.

The right job will make use of your natural talents and abilities. If they come from your Power Source, don't you think there is a good reason that you have them? You can make good money by using those talents. Remember your Power Source has ways and means that you know nothing of. Don't put confidence in how you think your dream will come to pass, but in the wondrous workings of God that can overpower all else.

I find your lack of faith disturbing. - Darth Vader, "Star Wars" (movie)

Share the Wealth

Request: Tell about a time you stepped out on faith to follow a dream.

"I left a marriage after 20 years with a psychopathic bully. Once I allowed my faith to carry me, I found myself with an abundance of everything that was lacking in that relationship: self-esteem, finances, career, love, etc." - *Sunshine*

"Doing it now. I have run my own business for eight years and I am writing my first novel." - *Rebecca*

"The last time I stepped out on faith is...Right Now! Finally I've decided to put my ambitions, dreams, and desires on the line with God and He told me that He's got me covered." - *SaseeDiva*

"I'd been working for nearly four years at a dreadful place in the Washington, D.C. area (I won't name this modern-day plantation, a radio station). Don't get me wrong, God tremendously blessed me while there, but I'd come to this station to pursue my dream of an on-air career, and found that I was being overlooked time and time again. I gave quite a bit of prayer to it and decided I was going to step out on faith and simply leave...and not just the job, but D.C. also. Within an extremely short period of time, I left, moved to Atlanta and continued to earnestly pray and believe for a nice entry-level on-air radio job. Four months later, God, being who He is, blessed me with not an entry-level radio job, but rather fulltime Midday Host [position] with a top Urban AC radio station in Chattanooga, TN. Bottom line...if you step out on faith, He'll handle the rest." - *Rabiyah*

"I will have my first art show in New York this year [2004]." - *The Anonymous Artist*

"I was married to a terrorist. He had been my only love and I thought that all men did not wash their balls. He was my sun and I revolved around him. I did everything I could, loved him the way I could, but he was still a terrorist. Finally, I jumped the slave ship, went through the Underground Railroad and *I'se free*! Therefore, I tell every woman who's in a bad relationship: Jump the slave ship! Drop the shackles! There is freedom waiting outside the stinky balls!" - *Lola*

"It was a long time ago when I was in the seventh grade. I was young but I was strong. I wanted to become the valedictorian of my eighth grade class the following year. My friends were only concerned with their boyfriends of the week and lip gloss. When I focused on my goal and stepped away from my comfort zone, which was being young and stupid, my friends disowned me. They accused me of being 'stuck-up' and 'brand-new'. They couldn't understand that studying and achieving my goal was more important than a party. I cried and prayed every day until I got up enough strength to continue by myself. By the next year, I realized I didn't need a whole group of friends/enemies holding me back. Independently, I accomplished my goal of being No. 1 in my class and I couldn't have been happier. It was worth the strife and ridicule." - *Samantha*

"I had a relatively easy job with the benefit of receiving cash money every week, the ability to come and go as I pleased throughout the work day, and very informal bosses. Though I was thankful to have such a gravy train, I was constantly feeling as though I wasn't living up to my potential. At one point during my employment, my first novel was published and I desperately wanted to devote my full attention to MY dream and not my bosses'. This mentality began to make it extremely difficult for me to show up for work on time, do what I was told, and get along with my coworkers. With no money saved - and rent that needed to be paid - I gave my boss a month's notice that I would be quitting to concentrate on my writing career.

"As my quitting date neared, I began to wonder if I had made the right decision. I prayed earnestly, said chosen affirmations hundreds of times a day, and took a really foolish, childlike approach to believing in miracles. With one week to go and no rent money for the next month, I was on the verge of suicide thinking that my life was not worth living if I couldn't make enough money being my own boss. Out of the blue, I got a phone call from my lawyer about an accident settlement. I had been told it would take a year after the accident for me to get the money; instead it had taken only six months - right on time for me to desperately need it. I immediately planned a book tour and have been my own boss since." - *Tahira*

Buttercup: We'll never survive.
Westley: Nonsense. You're only saying that because no one ever has.
-from "The Princess Bride" (movie)

Choose Your Own Attitude

Be very selective when obtaining career advice from others. People who are not happy with their jobs may or may not intentionally draw you into their misery by imparting one of these limiting beliefs.

People may tell you:

"Your job is supposed to suck from Monday through Friday so you can really enjoy your weekends."

"You don't have enough education to enjoy what you do for a living."

"You don't have enough experience to enjoy what you do for a living."

"You are supposed to hate your job because of the mistakes of Adam, Eve, Cain and Abel."

"Nobody likes his/her job. Why should you be any different?"

Even Queens who are happy with their means of income and their amount of income face adversity from people around them. The people criticizing these Queens value material possessions above experiencing spiritual fulfillment.

At the same time, people who are happy with their jobs (especially in your field of interest) may or may not intentionally give you limiting advice out of deep down insecurity that your career bliss will somehow lessen theirs. As Queens of the Universe, we are getting out of the habit of letting other people's beliefs determine the course of our lives.

QUEEN'S RULE: NOBODY TELLS ME WHAT MY CAREER GOAL SHOULD BE BECAUSE I AM INTELLIGENT AND BRAVE ENOUGH TO DECIDE FOR MYSELF.

If you send up a weather vane or put your thumb up in the air every time you want to do something different, to find out what people are going to think about it, you're going to limit yourself. That's a very strange way to live. – Jessye Norman, Opera and Jazz singer and humanitarian

Try this!

Hypnotize yourself!

What do you want to be?

a millionaire?
a famous artist?
an international singing sensation?
the owner of your own business?
happy?
supervisor?
loved by everyone?

Part of getting what you want is conducting yourself as though you already have it. When in situations, think to yourself, "What would a millionaire do in this situation?" "What would a person who is loved by everyone do in this situation?" Ignore what you see with your eyes... create a new picture with your mind – one in which you are what you want to be and very happy and thankful that you have realized your dream.

The eye is a coward. - African Proverb (Kenya)

The key to life is imagination. If you don't have that, no mater what you have, it's meaningless. If you do have imagination...you can make feast of straw. - Jane Stanton Hitchcock, author

Inspiration, not Envy

A queen can benefit greatly from others' success stories and how they overcame great odds in order to meet their goals. Not only do many celebrities have very inspirational life stories, but many people in our neighborhoods do as well. We come across many hurdles in our quest for success and in these times, we usually see no way over or around the discouraging circumstances. Somebody else's story of overcoming obstacles, lack of funds or plain old self-doubt just may propel a Queen to keep going when she thinks all is lost.

Saying, "If they can do it, so can I," does not have to project jealousy and bitterness. It should be a sign of hope and faith. Do not compare yourself to others as if you are somehow not good enough to achieve what they have or as if you are in competition. You have your own set of goals to accomplish, even if you don't know what they are. There is enough money and success for everyone in the world – especially those people who believe it is theirs to have.

Someone's success may seem to have come simply from his or her looks or their family's money. That doesn't mean you should compare your looks or your family's money to theirs. Not only do you have your own unique talents and abilities, you have a totally different road to travel than anyone else does. Your "lucky break" may come through a family friend, being in the right place at the right time, or some other miracle you couldn't possibly imagine. Does that mean you don't deserve the success?

When you learn of the great achievements of others, be careful not to force a feeling of unworthiness onto yourself. It is safe to let the success of others inspire you while you are giving yourself the encouragement you need to get things accomplished. Don't allow negative feelings toward others keep you from experiencing the best that Life can offer you.

Make It Happen!

Go with every off-the-wall, brilliant idea you have! You can feel it when it comes. The idea is so perfect that it scares you. Such ideas scare most of us so much that we talk ourselves out of them, insisting that, "it could never happen." Put extra thought into those ideas; write a game plan. Get the ball rolling even if it's just making a phone call or doing a little research via the library, internet or someone who went with one of *their* crazy ideas!

Don't scoff at other people's big ideas with a "Who does she think she is?" attitude. They are not stealing your spotlight. Remember: *The Universe is infinite.* Not only can your power never run out, there is enough power for others to step up to the throne and claim theirs.

Luke Skywalker: Alright, I'll give it a try.
Yoda: No! Try not. Do... or do not. There is no try.
- from "Star Wars: Episode V - The Empire Strikes Back" (movie)

Sex and your career

Many women stress over making names for themselves and gaining respect in the male dominated industries in which they work. It's a guarantee that SEX is not the way - unless, of course, you're a porn star. You may make a name for yourself but it won't be a good one.

You probably have men hitting on you all the time. Remember, they're men and you're the Queen of the Universe. Of course they want you. Let them grovel and drool; you don't have to oblige them. Allow them no other choice but to see you as a woman who is serious about her business. That garners more respect for what you have to offer to your particular field. Make a choice. Do you want sex or respect from the males you have to work with?

Make sure that when you walk into a career related meeting or business function, you as a topic of conversation won't end with, "I had her, too." Be forewarned: Men who see you as a good girl will try almost anything to infiltrate the fortress. It's all about hunting and conquering. Watch it!

Women who seek to be equal with men lack ambition.
– Timothy Leary, psychologist, philosopher and author

Queen of the Universe vs. The Peasant

The peasant slithers the office/workplace like a scavenger. She begs for everything from everybody. Today she examines your lunch and asks, "Can I taste that?" Tomorrow it'll be, "Let me borrow your pen for a sec," knowing that she has no intention on giving it back. Yesterday it was, "You got five dollars?"

The way she carries herself makes you wonder if she really works for a living. She may as well be panhandling in front of the building instead of collecting a check as an employee. You do not have to feel obligated to give to this leech – even if she's your supervisor. Never be afraid to say no to someone. It's possible to lovingly allow someone to be independent.

Also, reject the habit of asking your coworkers for anything unless it's detrimental to your work performance or job duties and in their job description to provide you with it. You know the difference. If you have to get one of those pens that hang around your neck on a string, then do it. Protect your food, money and supplies. It can't really hurt your employment; you'll be known as a person who is serious about her work and that's always a plus at any job.

Don't be the office bum!

But God bless the child that's got his own... that's got his own. He just worry 'bout nothin'... 'cause he's got his own. - Billie Holiday, "God Bless the Child" (song)

The Queen Takes On...
The Evil Coworker

DO: React to the person's ignorant comments as if he or she was standing in front of you naked picking his or her nose.

DON'T: Get into a bunch of arguments with them in front of other coworkers or the boss.

DO: Try to get stuff on tape, on paper, on film. Present it to your boss at a carefully planned moment or if things get too out-of-hand.

DON'T: Report them to the boss more than once a month. It'll make *you* look like the troublemaker.

DO: Do the best job that you can do, going above and beyond. Simply BE better than the evil coworker.

DON'T: Sabotage their work like they try to sabotage yours.

DO: Be more of a friendly loner at work. You're the Queen of the Universe. Everybody will want to be on your side, even the boss.

DON'T: Try to make friends and allies with everyone at work. You are there to work – period.

DO: Be the strong, silent Queen. Coworkers will be

intrigued by your mysterious ways.

DON'T: Gossip too much about them to others. (You can be sure that the same people who gossip *with* you are the same ones gossiping *about* you.)

DO: Have faith that what goes around comes around and that the person's bad ways have no power over your career.

DON'T: Lose your cool. That's what the evil coworker wants you to do.

QUEEN'S RULE: IF A WELL-MEANING BUT CONFUSED WOMAN SAYS THAT "BITCH" IS AN ACRONYM FOR "BEING IN TOTAL CONTROL OF HERSELF," I'LL LET HER KNOW: THE POWER SOURCE IN ME CONTROLS THE WHOLE UNIVERSE.

Many have had their greatness made for them by their enemies.
– Baltasar Gracian, Spanish philosopher and writer

HER KING

(Can also be titled "The Penis as Your Scepter"
if you're in a fun mood.)

If you feel that you always attract the wrong types of men, then you must change yourself in order to change the types of men who come into your life. You deserve a good, healthy relationship and there is such a thing as a relationship with no drama. Couples may have issues to work through every now and then, but that is the point of finding someone whose little quirks you can deal with the easiest.

If it excites you to argue, fight, stalk men or treat your relationships like the bumper car ride at your favorite amusement park... admit it to yourself and stop wondering why your relationships don't work out. You are not ready for a peaceful, healthy relationship. But, that is your choice and it is up to you and you only to decide when you want the cycle of unnecessary drama to end. Until then, you will only attract men who keep you where you want to be: in fights, arguments, confusion, and misery.

The following segment is for Queens who are ready to invite peace, harmony and TRUTH into every aspect of their lives, including romance. Read what the focus group guys have to say. You may not agree with their answers, but if it's you versus them, wrong versus right, then who is HAPPY? Only men can tell you what men are thinking. We can learn from what they say and use the information to our benefit or change teams altogether. The "Kings Speak" answers are not for us to agree or disagree with; they are for us to know the TRUTH about how men feel about us so that we may be better equipped to deal with them.

In this case, decide whether you truly want to understand where men are coming from. Wouldn't you like a peek inside of the male mind? We always want men to express themselves but rarely are we willing to hear the truth about how they really feel.

Before continuing with this segment of the book, you must decide:

Do you want to keep believing what you think you know about men or do you want the truth?

Do you want to unlock the mysteries of the male mind or do you want to continue to accept the lies told to you by yourself, your friends, "romance" entertainment, and men who simply tell you what you want to hear?

Do you want to attract the best man for you or do you want to continue fighting for different men who were never good enough for you in the first place?

Are you willing to change yourself or do you want the dreadful and impossible task of trying to change the men you meet?

Queen Theme: "Love Of Your Own" by Average White Band

Women would rather be right than reasonable. – Ogden Nash, American humorous poet

10 Facts about Men

Fact 1: All men are not the same. (Please hold your laughter.)

Let go of all your negative generalizations about men. They love to think that they are not all the same – and they are not - but even though they all closely resemble a little too strangely for their own good, we can give the Universe a chance to send us the right ones for us. The man who may be the total loser on your roster of past losers is the perfect man for someone else. Disgusting, but true.

Fact 2: Most men don't believe in platonic relationships.

These particular misguided creatures think that in a male-female friendship, at least one person is attracted to the other and would upgrade the relationship to a sexual one given the right opportunity. They don't get the fact that they could never, ever sleep with you if they were the last men on earth. Most of the men in your world think that they haven't slept with you yet because of some minor technicality that can be overcome someday. If it ever did begin to seep into their minds that you do not have any sexual feelings toward them – you would be thereby branded a lesbian. By the way… even if they KNOW that you are a lesbian, they still think they have a shot.

Nonetheless, it is important to have friendships with men – even if they seem to have no place in your Life. Like anybody else, they like to feel useful. Throw them a couple of adjectives like, "strong," "manly," and "ruggedly handsome" and allow them to help you out with some things like car repair and home improvement projects. They may actually turn out to be better friends than the women you know. Most of all... LISTEN to these men and what they talk about. Realizing what's important to Mr. Platonic might help you when seducing Mr. Loverman.

Remember, it is up to YOU to keep a relationship platonic. A man is not a platonic friend simply because you have not slept with him. If you flirt with him and tease him, he has reason to believe that he will have sex with you one day and that he is entitled to "more than friends" behavior. Women must form actual alliances with men that amount to more than flirting. Be open to having non-biological brothers and fathers without constantly overworking the damsel in distress role. These bonds should make you wiser when dealing with men because you can study and learn their thoughts and behaviors while in the comfort of a neutral zone.

I'm dating a woman now who, evidently, is unaware of it. – Garry Shandling, comedian

Fact 3: A lot of the men who don't call after asking for your number usually never intended to call.

First of all, why do women waste so much time on the question of why men don't call? Where's the dignity, the self-respect, or all the other guys you date? A Queen should be otherwise occupied or at least have her phone ringing so much that she doesn't notice who didn't call! A man's request for your phone number is not a guarantee that he is single and available. Many of the men "out on the prowl" have dire wife/girlfriend/kids/live-in lover commitments but they need to feel as if they can still attract women. Getting phone numbers is simply an ego boost. Also, consider this next fact...

Fact 4: Men actually *are* like dogs.

No, not in the sense that they'll hump anything. They are like dogs in the fact that they smell fear and it makes them act all crazy-like. There are very few things about women that men can sense or interpret, but your fear of loneliness or a desire for a serious relationship comes through loud and clear. Upon getting these scary vibes from a woman, a man starts to feel suffocated and he will squirm, wiggle and kick his way to breathing freely. This is true whether you just smiled at him in the grocery store or you've been dating him for a while.

Remember: Men aren't mind readers and most can't sense a woman's anger, aggravation, need to be held, dislike of his friends or family, fake sexual enthusiasm, or her attraction to another man. Still, there is nothing like a woman's fear of loneliness and desire for a serious relationship to set off a man's alarm. He won't play the superhero role and try to save her... he'll run like he stole something.

Fact 5: Men are not above trying to "trap" women.

You've heard about and seen the women who get pregnant on purpose, with the intent of holding onto a man. If a man feels threatened by your social life, career, or how well you may do without him... his ego may drive him to try and impregnate you. Like many men, he may feel that impregnating you not only bonds you to him for life, but also brands you as his woman forever. The point is to make you as undesirable as possible to other men while inconveniencing your social life and career. He may feel as if a baby would have you somehow dependent on him. Notice, the word MARRIAGE has nothing to do with it. A man doesn't have the same qualms as a woman does about marriage and kids going hand in hand. See Fact 6...

Fact 6: Men can very boldly, unashamedly, passionately and unapologetically separate marriage from fatherhood.

In other words, a man can separate a woman from the children he has by her. The average man wants children. Children are a way to boost his ego and make him feel as if he's left his mark on the world (and on a woman or two). They also usually provide him with a source of unconditional love and whatever sentimental reasons that women usually give for wanting children. The important thing to know here is that his wanting children does not mean that he wants the woman who will have them for him.

As women, we've been taught that marriage and kids go hand-in-hand. Though many women have embarked on the brave journey of single motherhood by their OWN decision, a lot of us would still prefer a happy marriage to complete the package. What we must learn to do is separate men's desire for children from their desire for us. They've already made the distinction; it's time for us to catch up. (Also see page 146 for more information on waking up to men's true intentions.)

Fact 7: Men can be gold diggers too.

It's a new day, a new century, a new millennium. In general, men are coming to terms with the possibility of their women making more money than they do. As a matter of fact, quite a few men would love to meet a woman who makes more money so that they can attach themselves and fulfill the material desires of their hearts. They'll see no harm in planning ventures with your money, especially if they can woo you with the gift of gab, a handsome face, or explosive sexual prowess.

Their job is to get you to love them so that they can accomplish their goals. Many of these men feel that women have too long gotten away with being supported by men and that it's the men's turn to sit back and be taken care of. Use caution when disclosing your financial well-being (and see page 135 for more information on when he's only after your cash).

Fact 8: Not all men prefer skinny women.

Many will take a woman just as she is, as long as she has confidence, good self-esteem and the type of personality he likes. There are lots of men who prefer women "with meat on their bones". Weight should play a factor in your health, not your relationship. If you find that it is becoming an issue in your relationship, then drop the extra weight – HIM.

Fact 9: There are men who like women with hair on their bodies.

Legs, underarms and bikini areas are shaved very often. However, there are many men who don't mind it. If you're one of those Queens who prefers to venture 'in the natural', then don't be afraid to be different. Sure, your dream guy may come from another country, but there are plenty takers in the good old U.S. of A.

A King Speaks:
"Leg hair is natural. I don't like when a woman shaves her pubic hair. Only little girls have no pubic hair. I like knowing that I'm with a real woman." - Mark

Fact 10: Men need compliments and appreciation just as much as women do.

They don't need this as often as we do, but they love to feel as if they are somehow making our lives easier. Men have been taught that they should be providers and that they have to be emotionally and physically stronger than women. In doing our part to maintain loving, healthy relationships, we should be on the watch for when they exert themselves in a show of how well they can provide for us. If he is doing something right, whether it's in his great fathering skills, his handy work around the house, cooking a great meal, or making you tingle between the sheets... he wants to know that he is doing it right!

Each man has his own way of proving his strength, intelligence and ability to provide, so not every way is good for every woman. But if you find that man who just does that thing in that way you love so much... LET HIM KNOW! Don't forget those compliments. If he has a particular shirt that looks especially good on him, tell him. If you're with him in a setting that includes other men trying to compete for the title of "Top Dog" (i.e. a party, a sporting event, any kind of reunion, or even a work-related function), tell him how much better he is in some way than the other men in the room. Keep your gushing under control, though... too much and you'll scare him.

Man forgives woman anything save the wit to outwit him. - Minna Thomas Antrim, writer, from *Naked Truths and Veiled Illusions*

The Single Queen

Meeting His Royal Highness

Don't focus so much on the physical. There may be different physical features about a man that turn you on, but you may meet a thousand who fit that description and treat you horribly. You deserve more from a relationship. By not being especially shallow, you will open your possibilities and find a man whose total being is so attractive that you'll forget that he only has one of the physical traits that you think you value so highly. If you keep an open mind and trust your Power Source to bring you only the best, you may even find someone who has all the physical traits you want plus the mental and emotional ones you need.

Give guys a chance instead of brushing them off so quickly. This does not include various drunks, weirdos or criminals who may cross your path. You're a smart woman – you know when a guy is definitely not worth your time. However, when a guy comes to you correctly (whichever way you think that is), don't discount him for things that really don't matter such as height, weight, race, etc. Don't count him out because of his job, either. The guy behind the counter at the hardware store may be everything you want in a man and more. You don't have to give everyone your phone number or invite everyone to your home, but you can change your whole mindset to be a tad friendlier when meeting new people.

Even though first impressions last, don't judge a book by its cover. Just because he is dressed in a suit and tie doesn't mean he is employed or in his right mind. He may be driving a nice car at the moment, but do you know if it's his? Don't be fooled by dirty work boots and stained pants that could easily be worn by a successful man who just finished construction on his own house. A briefcase could be empty, protecting the want-ads or carrying drug paraphernalia. A man exiting a house of worship could've been in there stealing money or raping someone. Dirty nails don't imply slobbery. They also imply a Mr. Fix-It with his own business, money and free time. Look before you leap (at him or away from him).

Some women think that a man who only gives his pager, cell or work number upon introduction is hiding something – like a wife. Consider this: He may want to be sure you're going to call him before giving you full access to him. There are crazy women out there and he needs to weed them out just as you need to weed out the crazy men. If, however, you've been on several dates and he still doesn't give up a home number and you still don't know where he lives... beware. No need to pester him for the info. He should give it up voluntarily. If not, you have to decide if you would like to continue seeing him and accepting less than what you really want and deserve.

Want to find the right King for you? Stop looking. Don't put up an "All men are dogs" or an "I'm too good for you" wall. The best men can spot it and it turns them off. (Plus, you'll miss out on all kinds of advantages that women get from men for just being women.) Be pleasant and cool. That can't hurt anyone.

Many, many women avoid relationships with men because of the pain they suffered at the hands of just one or two jerks. That's right... just one or two. There are billions of men on this planet and they stopped after one or two couldn't give them the Love they deserved. Lady, are you a Queen or what? Does a Queen not DESERVE a loving relationship? And why should you remain bored and unappreciated forever because your independent butt convinced yourself that your vibrator is just as good as the real thing? Oh, that's right - vibrators don't come with drama. They also can't fix you an early morning/late night breakfast. And Queens of the Universe deserve breakfast! Don't let the jerks have that much control over your life. Make room in your heart for a loving relationship NOW!

Men act and women appear. Men look at women. Women watch themselves being looked at. - John Berger, actor and critic

KINGS SPEAK

Question: How can a woman flirt with a man she wants to become acquainted with and not appear cheap or desperate?

Patrick:
"1. INITIATE: Don't be afraid to initiate a conversation or to initiate a new topic when already engaged.
2. ENGAGE: Be an equal partner in a conversation... This means listen, ask questions, and assert your opinion. If you don't like what you hear, you can always move on.
3. LAUGH: Don't be afraid to laugh... men like it as much as women, even if we have dumber jokes. Don't be afraid to be embarrassed. Be nice, but tell a joke, poke fun, pick a topic, compliment. Don't worry if you'll look stupid - a guy is just happy to have the attention.
4. TOUCH: Touch his arm or hand... no need to start sloppy kisses, but touch shows romantic interest.
5. BE SELECTIVE: If you don't like what you hear, or the conversation goes places that you don't want to go...bail out and move on."

Greg:
"I am not a super-duper intellectual; I am an intellectual with a personality. How can a woman meet me on that level of intellect and personality? I'll respect you more because you are able to provide something other than, 'You have a sexy body,' or 'I like your car.' Talk to me about social concerns but at the same time, have a personality where we can laugh and joke about people. Have a conversation about the election but crack a joke about how we make decisions about the leadership of this country."

Kareem:
"The best way to flirt with a man is to be pleasant and nice. EVERY MAN loves a woman who is pleasant. Also smile and compliment the small things like a man's hair cut or his shoes."

Dave:
"Don't act like you're God's gift by playing hard to get and ignoring men around you. The simplest thing a woman can do to flirt is to make eye contact with a man, smile and/or speak. That's all she has to do."

Shuges:
"To each his own, but touching, eye contact and certain facial gestures can be very stimulating in a subtle way. And anything subtle is hard to be labeled 'trashy'. Now... flirting with a man's buddy or co-workers is a definite no-no! THAT is cheap and trashy.
Of course once you get to KNOW your man, then nothing is cheap or trashy! A skirt with no undies? No prob."

Michael James:
"By looking into his eyes and showing interest in his mind."

Kevin:
"I think if we're talking about strangers, women can flirt just by being friendly. It seems like women are always prepared to dis somebody, and men (at least the ones I know) expect attitude when we approach women. If we're talking about a co-worker, a friend of a friend or some other acquaintance, touching is a good way. I don't mean anything suggestive, but when a woman is talking and she puts her hand on my shoulder or laughs and leans my way, I kinda know that she would be receptive to me asking her out."

Roc:
"Approach a man the way you want a man to approach you. Great come on lines: 'Nice shirt, tie, cologne.' Express a compliment without putting yourself on rejection notice. Keeping up the conversation is also a smart move. Ask open-ended questions: Where did you go to school? Did you like it? Why/why not? If you ask about the job, you're presumed to be a gold digger. Spitfire questions are tacky. The best way to pick up a guy: Friendly convo, friendly convo, friendly convo... But let your eyes do the real talking."

(Remaining Anonymous):
"I think a woman should be herself and still flirt, but in a respectable manner. They shouldn't leave the door open for something that they can't get out of but while flirting, they should choose what they say very carefully. If you tease a wolf, he will attack!"

Kato:
"Basically, by showing genuine interests in the things in his world/atmosphere."

Slick:
"A little smile goes a long way! So does good conversation."

DeLano:
"It's all in the approach. If there is a man out there that you are interested in and you want to garner his interest, ask him out to dinner, coffee, museum, etc. and make the event about you. Go to your favorite restaurant, invite him along and just have a good conversation and good fellowship. I don't think any man could mistake that for 'cheap/easy'. If you want to avoid being embarrassed in person... email is a very acceptable form of communication. Send him an email with what you have planned and

go from there."

Elliott:
"Be honest and straightforward. This may only work with REAL MEN."

A man:
"Don't play with your tongue in front of him. Show interest by asking him personal stuff like you really want to know - stuff that only women who are interested would want to know."

Eben:
"No woman who flirts with me is cheap. I only hope to be good enough to warrant a flirt, especially from a woman I may be interested in."

I'm a guy, I don't stop! The woman's supposed to stop. We're the gas, they're the brakes! - Ray, "Ed TV" (movie)

Whatcha Really Want

If you only want a quick fling, do what you think you need to in order to accomplish that goal. Same goes if you're looking for an on-going, indefinite sexual relationship. However, if you're a woman who usually falls for a guy after getting sexually involved, you should know better than to attempt any meaningless trysts. Don't try to imitate the hard-hearted women you've become acquainted with in songs, movies, TV or your circle of friends. You're only lying to yourself and you'll end up hurt. Let other women do what they can handle; it doesn't mean that you have to follow suit. Be true to yourself.

If marriage or a long-term meaningful relationship is your goal, there is another set of rules to follow. For thousands of years, Queens who are aware of their special power have been able to attract the men they wanted. Part of the key to this feat has always been making the man feel as if it was his decision to choose her, even though by all intelligent accounts, it is the woman who chooses the man. This "lends" him some power.

Men love to feel as if they are in control – it helps them feel like MEN. There is an art to this and it's actually much easier and yields better results than behaving in an undignified manner to get a man's *temporary* attention.

A Case for Chastity

Men seem to enjoy sex and/or have an orgasm 99% of the time - regardless of partner or circumstance. On the contrary, a woman's sexual fulfillment and enjoyment depends on her partner in said encounter, the circumstances surrounding their relationship and the encounter itself - including details such as foreplay and penis size (to name a few). For some women, the choice to limit sexual partners is simply about fairness. These women have taken a stand in pleasure. They want to be sure that they will actually *enjoy* the sex that they have or that a man would be worth training if his skills aren't up to par. In weeding out potential duds-in-the-sack, their choices in sexual partners are reduced significantly. Consequently, their "I Wish I Hadn't" lists are not as long as most and they enjoy more meaningful relationships. Just an FYI with a wink.

If pussy was a stock, it would be plummeting right now because you've flooded the market with it. You give it away too easy. - Dave Chappelle, actor and comedian, from "Killin' Them Softly" (HBO)

The Lost Art of the Proper Flirt

The Old School Flirt
It is the woman who chooses the man who will choose her. - Paul Geraldy

Give him a small, friendly smile and make it sincere. Use your eyes. They're usually a Queen's best feature, contrary to what most of us think. Let your eyes and smile tell him that you are interested but not desperate. When you catch his glance, let your eyes do the talking. One glance can say, "I'm interested in you and I'd like to know more."

All meaningful looks should be confident, not desperate. Would a Queen have to beg? A three-second gaze will do the trick. Then, give a sly smile and go on about your business. He'll come to you if he's interested. If he's a shy guy, you may have to make the first move. Be confidently friendly, not aggressive.

Slim Pickin's
There certainly are not so many men of large fortune in the world as there are of pretty women to deserve them. - Jane Austen, author

Sometimes you're in an environment with what old-timers call "slim pickin's" during which, at least ten women will go after the same one or two guys. This is one of the most frequent and destructive causes of division between women. Queens can't let this happen. Your motto is, "Thy will be done," an affirmation to your Power Source that if you're meant to become acquainted with anyone, you will be. Do your Old School Flirt and trust that whatever happens is in your best interest.

When the other women shamelessly do any and every thing to get attention, you must keep your cool. You'll actually stand out from the rest by conducting yourself as royalty. See if the men are smart enough to come up and introduce themselves. If not, it's their loss and you don't want a man who isn't wise enough to see a good thing when it's right in front of him.

A Flirt's Uniform
I could depend a lot on my shaking, though I never shimmied vulgarly and only to express myself. – Ethel Waters, singer and actress

You've been complimented on your breasts, legs, tummy or buns? Congratulations, you're a woman. You're not the first and you won't be the last. Men have made a fun game for themselves of guessing what we look like naked. Many pride themselves on being able to do this no matter what a woman is wearing.

Why take away their fun and valuable thinking time by showing them everything at once? Men are very attracted to a sense of mystery in a woman. This is another way for you to maintain power while making them feel as if they have some. Let them imagine what's under that smashing outfit. Won't they feel smart? Challenged? Accomplished? Sure, they will. But they need your help. And that guy who's passed the "He's Worth a Try" Test… what a nice surprise you'll be able to give him on your first unveiling.

Every now and then a Queen needs her ego boosted, her spirits lifted, her hormones rejuvenated. She puts on a Look-At-These top and a Don't-This-Look-Yummy skirt just for a Pick-Me-Up. Pun intended. Use these types of outfits sparingly if you're in the market for a serious relationship. If you are comfortable at this point in your life with just being looked at as the good time girl, there's nothing wrong with that. Just as long as you know what you want and are ready for the consequences. Our society has made it extremely difficult for a woman to be respected as a Queen if she was once known to 'get around'.

You know those guys who work out waaaay too much or spend an excessive amount of time on their looks because they're overcompensating for a lack of brains, talent, money or a basic personality? There are women like that, too. Indecent exposure of their bodies or major use of makeup gives most men the impression that women are overcompensating. Men will come and go (literally) because they've already made up their minds about these women and won't give them the chance to prove that they have other qualities besides a killer body.

There are clothes you can wear that will show off your curves and still provide a respectable look. Make your decision. Do I want to attract men who drool over any pair of exposed boobs, buns or gams? Or do I want to attract men who are interested in the whole woman? A *QUEEN to be exact.*

I'm not bad, I'm just drawn that way. - Jessica Rabbit, "Who Framed Roger Rabbit" (movie)

Share the Wealth

Question: How can a woman draw the line between being sexy and being trashy with her clothes and attitude?

"Sexiness comes from an attitude that is confident and self-assured. Sexy women don't have to wear next-to-nothing, but a little v-neck here, a split there just to show a peak of skin is sexy. 'Leaving it to their imagination.' Subtle flirtatious gestures are sexy." - *Samantha*

"Don't chance letting those puppies (i.e., breasts) fall out." - *Terri*

"When you show it all, there's nothing left to the imagination. You look like you're saying, 'Hey y'all! Look! Look at me!' Sophistication in subtle, sexy clothes is a classy act." - *Sunshine*

"A woman can be sexy by just loving herself. When she loves herself, she automatically becomes sexy because when she walks into a room, she carries herself a certain way. Leave something for the imagination and as my big sis told me, 'Whores bend, ladies stoop.' <hearty laugh>" - *Lola*

"Less is definitively not the sexiest way to dress. Classy and feminine is alluring, yet decent and not tacky. Not too much cleavage, thigh and not so tight you cannot breathe, sit or bend over!" - *Rebecca*

"Confidence (sexiness) is knowing that you don't have to prove yourself. Arrogance (trashiness) is always feeling the need to prove (or should I say fool) yourself." - *SasseeDiva*

"Don't try to be the woman that men want to have sex with. Be the woman they want to marry." - *Tahira*

"[Wearing] clothes that fit is a really good start! But after that, it's all about colors and pheromones. Do the clothes make you feel good? Then feeling sexy is next. I do not believe SPANDEX feels good on anybody." - *Michelle*

Long Live the Chase

Sometimes I wonder if men and women really suit each other. Perhaps they should live next door and just visit now and then.
– Katharine Hepburn, actress and writer

It's the chase. We all love it, whether we are mature enough to admit it or not. Call it a challenge or the forbidden fruit cliché, but males and females are highly attracted to what it seems they cannot have. How many times have you thought a boyfriend changed since you first met him? Well, he already got you into bed and a relationship. What's there to work for?

A man who really wants to be with you will work not only to get you, but also to **keep** you. Queens of the Universe are worth keeping and they know it. There's no room for insecurity, for it shows all too well in a relationship. Your being insecure tells a man that you don't think you are worthy of keeping. With this attitude, why should *he* think you are worthy of keeping?

Some men will never know the worth of a Queen until they lose one or two. Some go through their whole lives losing good women until they find themselves old and lonely. If you run across a man like this, let him go. No need to convince him how worthy you are of love and a good relationship. The right man for you will realize that by himself, in his own time. Would the Queen of the Universe need to chase a man or try to prove her worth? No way! She's the Queen of the Universe. Actually, men are constantly trying to prove themselves to her.

The Bedroom War

Women are forced into committing sexual acts with men that violate integrity because the universal religion — contempt for women — has as its first commandment that women exist purely as sexual fodder for men. – Andrea Dworkin, author

People in our lives will only do what we let them do. They will only take what we give them. They will only go as far as we let them go. You don't have to accept disrespect and things that hurt your feelings or your body just to keep a man. Women have the power. Some men know this and accept it. They hold women in the high regard they deserve because they see the Divinity in themselves as well as in us. At the same time, there are men who don't see the Divinity in themselves, are carrying hurt from bad experiences, under the spell of media and entertainment or just mentally unstable. They are threatened by the power of a woman and spend their whole lives trying to shut it down. Sadly, they succeed more often than not. And now, shutting down a woman's Divine power is a worldwide movement.

Men have been making laws and rules that rob women of their human rights since the beginning of time. Now that most of the world has given women equal rights, there is an overwhelming movement designed to keep women in submission as sexual objects. They wouldn't be able to do this if we didn't let them.

Somewhere between entertainment and our bedrooms, the phrase "for entertainment purposes only" was lost. A reality check for Queens of the Universe:

You do not have to look like an airbrushed magazine image or a video girl (who usually gets *paid* to look like that) in order to get or keep a man.

You do not have to put up with a man's cheating. (He wouldn't put up with yours!)

You do not have to do anything that compromises your dignity or personal beliefs to please a man sexually.

This movement to keep women in sexual bondage has been affecting bedrooms, relationships and psyches all over the world where some men have led us to believe that we have to be outrageous sexual freaks in order to just barely hold their attention. Insecure men see these images in movies, read about escapades in magazines and hear in songs what a man should be able to get away with. He knows his chances of getting any of this in real life are slim to none unless he is a celebrity, has a lot of money to pay for it, or knows a crack whore.

Collectively, these insecure men make it their business to make us think that we owe them something. How ridiculous.

Think of the long-held belief that women should be virgins when they get married. Nobody makes too much of a fuss about men being virgins. Sounds like a rule created by men in different societies all over the world so you wouldn't be able to compare penis sizes. There is nothing wrong with being a virgin, of course. But for the woman who would like to safely explore her options, she should have that right without being ridiculed.

All men are not insecure. However, like any human being, they are going to go as far as they can, test limits and take exactly what you give them. If they can get you to bring their nastiest, most vile fantasies to life, they will. Your man may not intend to break up with you next week, next month, next year... but when he does, you'll feel like a fool because you compromised your morals to keep him and he didn't show his gratitude by staying with you.

Each Queen has her own preferences. Some are more over-the-top than others, but it is up to each Queen individually to decide what type of sex she should have, with whom and how often. If you are a Queen of the more kinky persuasion, don't wear your sexual habits on your sleeve. Save it for when you get the special person of your choice into the bedroom. If you flaunt your freaky ways, people get the impression that you're up for grabs and anyone can get a piece. The Queen carries herself in a way that shows how much respect she has for herself and her privacy.

Don't let anyone guilt trip you into sex that you are not comfortable with. There is a person out there for you who wants just what you want, or who is willing to go at your pace so that you both can learn from each other. In fact, you may get into serious relationships over the years with several men who complement you sexually. Like everything else we want in life, you have to believe that it is possible and that you deserve it.

If you are in a serious relationship and are concerned that you have no desire for sex (not including abstaining for religious reasons), you should consider that it might be an emotional or mental problem. You may have a mental or physical health issue that stems from past or present abuse or insecure feelings about yourself and sex. On the other hand, that particular relationship could be the problem. You may be with your partner for the wrong reasons and your body is taking a stand because you won't.
(Also see page 204 for information on how these issues cause vaginal infections.)

Women punish themselves for the failure to conform. – Sandra Bartky, professor, author

Reality Check: RAPE

Get it straight. No one has the right to violate you. No one has the right to have sex with you against your will. Rape is wrong and unacceptable.

Having understood that, we as Queens of the Universe need to be SMARTER. We cannot continue to put ourselves in potentially dangerous situations that can possibly lead to rape and sometimes, even murder.

When most of us leave our homes, we lock our doors. When we park our cars, we lock our doors (and in most cases use an anti-theft device). When we have casual sex, we use condoms. Recently, most of us have taken extra measures with bank accounts, credit cards and other personal information to prevent identity theft. Looking closely, we take precautions to avoid trauma in every aspect of our lives except the sexual aspect, which when damaged is usually even more mentally, emotionally and physically devastating than anything previously named.

If a Queen fails to lock her doors, activate an anti-theft device, use a condom or protect her personal information, you wouldn't say it was HER fault that she was burglarized, infected, or terrorized financially... OR WOULD YOU? Would you say that it was a woman's fault that she was a victim of date rape? Take some time to think about it.

Queens of the Universe are too smart not to take preventative measures for something as common as date rape, which usually goes unreported. At the times when this horrific crime is reported, the woman's sexual history, mental health history and general reputation is put on the line for something that – quiet as it's kept – is usually avoidable.

Date rape does not involve someone stalking you, kidnapping you, or jumping out at you from the bushes. It happens on dates, meaning the two people involved knew each other. In most cases, the woman trusted her attacker enough to go out with him and be alone with him.

Men and women think on totally different levels. This is not to lead you to believe that all men are capable of date rape. However, did you know that most date rape attackers really do believe that their victims wanted the sex? Most don't feel that they did anything wrong.

For the most part, a woman has already made up her mind about whether she would like to have sex with a man she has become acquainted with. She knows if he will remain "just a friend" or if he has potential for a sexual or long-term serious relationship. Often, she knows *when* she will have sex with a man, if ever. Sometimes, a man whom she expected to be "just friends" with turns out to have a chance for something more. On the other hand, a man who originally had a chance for sex will change her mind by not living up to her criteria for moving ahead to an intimate level.

Generally speaking, men are not as complex as we are. The whole fact that he asked you out means that he would like to have sex with you. The guys who agreed to remain friends with you would still have sex with you if given the opportunity. (There are a few exceptions, but again, we are generally speaking.)

Many women can and will accept dinners, gifts, dates and attention from men whom they have no romantic interest in. Lots of times, we feel comfortable enough with a male "friend" to hang out alone with him or even share the same bed. We appreciate the men who are attracted to us, but understanding enough to do things for us without expecting sex or a relationship. The reality of the situation is that 90% of the time, they are only doing these things in an attempt to change our minds about having sex or a relationship with them. What you see as a harmless agreement to be alone with such a man, he sees as a chance to have sex with you.

In spite of everything, it should be stated that all men are *not* animals who can't control their sexual desires. But keep in mind that all people who pass your house are not thieves waiting to break in. Yet, you lock your doors. You wear a seatbelt just in case you're in an accident. It's not because you believe that all of the cars on the road are just itching to smash into yours. There's something called PREVENTION. Be smart!

The following suggestions will be hard for some women to take into account. Unfortunately, a lot will learn the hard way that date rape is a very serious issue.

-Know who your TRUE (male) FRIENDS are. 'Platonic' does not mean 'friend'. If you feel that you have to run down a few rules to him before going out with him, he is not your true friend. He is a male whom you are trying to hold onto as 'platonic' even though you are aware of his attraction to you. It is possible for him to misconstrue your kindness as an invitation to sex.

-Know your alcohol limit and stick to it. Drugs and alcohol weaken your personal defense. Rapists (and men in general) count on drugs and alcohol to bring your guard down. No judgment on anyone's personal habits, but stick to a limit and/or travel with friends who will keep an eye on you at all times. Unless you know that a friend of yours plans to have sex with a man, do not allow her to go off alone with him. If you must, follow them so that you can be her backup if necessary.

-When on a date or anywhere that is not a family gathering, do not leave your food or drink unattended. People can slip you drugs very easily through your unwatched plate or glass. If a semi-stranger offers to bring you food or a drink, refuse politely and get it yourself.

-If you do not intend on having sex with a man, do not be alone with him. He may take it as a signal that you want to have sex. (Exception: your TRUE male FRIENDS). It doesn't do any good to set rules for the evening or tell him, "I'm going to your place, but I don't want to do anything." The fun for him is in the chase; he will just try to change your mind. Again, this does not mean that all men are ruthless animals. You don't know who the rapist is until he rapes you. What a horrible way to find out. If this suggestion isn't conducive to your lifestyle, please take self-defense classes or carry pepper spray - anything to protect yourself against an attack.

-WARN OTHERS! Preventing rape is as important as seatbelts, condoms, and door locks. Spread the word. Engage in discussions about rape with your girlfriends as well as the men you date. A man's opinion on rape can tell you a lot about him.

-Don't be so quick to agree to sex at a man's home or anywhere else you're not familiar with. Technology provides pervs with ways to videotape you and sometimes broadcast you without your knowledge. This is a "space age" rape. Also, a century of horrific news reports about women being abducted, abused and murdered by men they knew casually should make us think twice about every man we go out with. If you are into one-night stands, take him to a hotel. Bringing all of your dates back to your place could be hazardous. If you are dating someone whom you see as more than a fly-by-night partner and you don't feel comfortable enough to go to his home without suspecting foul play, then trust your instincts and get away from him.

-Teasing is neither cute nor fair to a man. Do not play with a man's emotions and hormones if you do not intend to sleep with him. If you tell him that he is a friend, keep it that way. It's easy for us to make guys think that we barely know the difference between innocent flirting, blatant teasing, or just being nice. Many times they don't know any better, but WE do. Women who intentionally tease guys make it difficult for other women. Teases fall into the drama queen category and are seeking attention. By dangling and snatching the possibility of sex, they feed their desire for attention and begin to feel a false sense of power over a man. Unfortunately, drama queens also seek sympathy. By putting themselves in dangerous situations, they are subconsciously seeking a tragedy that would cause people to have to come to their rescue and feel sorry for them.

As stated before, a lot of date rapists are not aware that they are rapists. In many cases, they are not mean people. They are weak men who find you attractive and use sex to validate their manhood and to feel powerful. That whole "she wanted it" defense comes from a man truly believing that you wanted to have sex, whether he's just that dense or fully convinced by his own ego.

Your sexual practices are up to you and you only, but don't underestimate your natural intuition. You deserve to date responsibly, safely and according to your own beliefs.

If you have been a victim of date rape or "space age" rape, do not blame yourself. It was a horrible situation that you did not deserve and it is okay to report it. Many women don't have the courage to come forth because they are holding on to self-blame. Let the self-blame go. It is very scary to know that a woman's sexual history is always put on trial instead of the behavior of the rapist and this stops most women from going forward with prosecution. Contact a rape crisis hotline or see a doctor or counselor and learn how to deal with it emotionally. You may be convinced to bring your attacker to justice.

It should also be noted that many women are raped by their husbands and boyfriends. Some men feel as if marriage or commitment entitles them to get sex from a woman whenever they want to, whether the woman is willing or not. Women who are in relationships with such men are often made to feel guilty for not performing their "duties". You do not have to have sex with anyone at any time if you are not a willing participant. A husband or a boyfriend does not have rights to your body. You do!

QUEEN'S RULE: I TAKE RESPONSIBILITY FOR MY LIFE AND MY ACTIONS.

The woman who rejects the stereotype of feminine weakness and dependence can no longer find much comfort in the cliché that all men are beasts. She has no choice except to believe, on the contrary, that men are human beings, and she finds it hard to forgive them when they act like animals. –Christopher Lasch, American Historian

Know the Difference

If he wants to see you or be with you, he will!

Men will take advantage of an opportunity to have a sexual relationship with no strings attached but in this day and age, most women appreciate that opportunity as well.

However, if you find that you are dating a guy whom you want to be exclusively yours... look for signs that he is up for a serious relationship.

Wants a relationship: He spends a lot of his leisure time with you.
Just screwing around: He's not willing to give you more than a few hours of his leisure time per week.

Wants a relationship: He makes an effort to DATE you and prove that he's not just interested in sex.
Just screwing around: You only get "booty calls" OR he tries to get some every time you see him.

Wants a relationship: He WANTS to pay for dates – with no guaranteed sex at the end of the night.*
Just screwing around: He's really into that "dutch" thing and still tries to get some at the end of the night.

Wants a relationship: He will TELL you that he wants to see you exclusively.**
Just screwing around: He often reminds you how great it is that you can have sex with no strings attached.

Wants a relationship: He usually calls you at least twice

a day (if long distance rates don't apply).***
Just screwing around: You do most of the calling.

*You should at least offer to pay if you are the one who invited him out. He has great "keeper" potential if he still refuses to let you pay.

**Be careful of the guy who wants you to be exclusively *his* but continues behavior showing that he's not exclusively *yours*.

***Beware of the man who calls you often, but only to keep tabs on you. Many will give you tentative plans every day just to keep you from going out with anyone else. The man who wants a relationship will be honest about when he can see you - and it will be often.

ALSO... You should be aware that many men who are already in situations (marriage, living with a woman, dating someone seriously) wouldn't mind carrying on a pseudo-serious relationship with you. They wouldn't feel the need to get a divorce, move out or break up with the woman they're with. They say, "It's complicated," and "These things take time." They will say things to evoke your sympathy while keeping you pacified with gifts, fun and compliments. What you don't get is the man himself. If you want a serious relationship with a man who is already in a "situation", then take nothing less. Be a platonic friend or leave him alone completely. That's the only way to find out if he is willing to be with you exclusively. Note: 'Exclusively' doesn't mean that you are the only *other* woman besides his wife or girlfriend.

Don't take no shit. If you take shit, you're gonna keep getting shit. And then they'll take a stick and stir it up for you.
- Denise Young, educator and mother

A Queen's Relationships

A Queen Infatuated or In Love ...possibly In Bondage

What Seem Like Well-Meaning, Very Supportive Actions That Screw Up Relationships

What you're doing: Looking for a man
Your intent: To find a man
What a man sees: You frantically, desperately searching for *any* man, screaming "I need to be loved!"

What you're doing: Being available all the time; Always being home whenever he gets there
Your intent: To show him that you are there for him; to prove that you aren't seeing anyone else
What a man sees: You wallowing in lonely misery because you have no life and nobody else wants you

What you're doing: Talking about the future (marriage, kids, a movie next week).
Your intent: To show him that you take him seriously
What a man sees: You crying because you think you'll grow old alone

What you're doing: Paying for almost every date and buying him presents all the time
Your intent: To show him you aren't after his money; to show him how independent you are
What a man sees: A woman he can take advantage of; a woman who thinks she has to buy love

What you're doing: Canceling plans for him
Your intent: To show him how important he is to you
What a man sees: A cool game of, "What can I get her to cancel for me this time?"

What you're doing: Trying to be perfect all of the time
Your intent: To keep him in love with you forever
What a man sees: A possibility that if he got a woman *that* good, he can find an even better one

Just as women are afraid of receiving, men are afraid of giving.
– John Gray, author

KINGS SPEAK

Question: What do you wish women would just *get* about men?

Roc:
"We're so simple it's scary. Feed me, f@#k me, shut up (especially when the game is on). Women make things complex. If we don't invite you out with us, you're not invited. Stop pouting."

Ben:
"I wish that women would get that men are really simple creatures. Also, what men will look at in videos or on the street is not what he actually is looking for in a girlfriend or wife."

DeLano:
"You can't change us. You maybe able to smooth out the rough spots (clean his nails, pick out a tie, pick up his socks) but wholesale changes are not going to happen. A man can't change his true self. If his nature is to be shiftless and lazy, then unless he makes the decision to do otherwise, he will continue to be shiftless and lazy.

"Consider this: If you have a dream to live a Lexus life and the man you have fallen in love with is a more of a 77 Cadillac type... Do you try to make him a Lexus dude against his will? (nope) Do you become a 77 Caddy girl (??) or try to find someone with whom you are evenly yoked? (Bingo!) So with that being said, accept us for who we are and don't be upset if we don't meet your expectations for us. Love us for who we are and be honest with yourself that you can't make a man be a man. He has to do that all on his own."

Slick:
"A man needs MAN TIME."

Mark:
"One thing women should get about men is that we are NOT the same gender, so don't try to make me what you feel I should be. You are looking at us from a female perspective. Remember, you played with Barbies while we played with Tonka trucks and GI Joes. Another thing women should get about men is that we like things to be as simple as possible. Don't over complicate things because that's when we start to panic, which can lead to fear of the relationship. Life is complicated, why make your relationship another complication?"

A man:
"Sometimes there are no lines to read in between."

Dave:
"I think women should just get the fact they we are all not liars and cheaters and all of the negative stuff they normally hear. I get tired of having that label but I guess throughout history we might have put that on ourselves."

Shuges:
"We're not mind readers! Whatever it is that's bothering you, let us know. Also, stop trying to make your man do something he does NOT want to do (visit in-laws, be nice to a neighbor who he obviously dislikes, etc). And finally, don't try to change your man. In other words, attempting to make him more like your brother, your father, your best friend - or even worse, your ex - is a HUGE no-no!"

Kevin:
"Everything in life does not revolve around her. If I take the call on my other line, that is not a rank of importance. I will not get rid of female friends because we really like

each other. Don't worry about if I told my mother that you said hi."

Greg:
"I don't need you to be my mother. Men are basically the way they are because for whatever reason, women feel that they can be that guide, that helper. If women can see that we don't need that mother, they can allow us to be men. Let us fall sometimes. We're gonnna be alright."

Kato:
"We're not the fucking enemy."

Patrick:
"We do not read minds. Doing things that you hope will get a particular result; taking actions you hope will signal your feelings; and not telling a man when something we do - or something that someone else has done - bothers her... These acts are generally doomed to failure. Women have to take responsibility for their feelings and show enough trust in their relationships to assert what is on their minds. And trust their men to be accepting of their feelings even if they don't agree or understand. Hoping for the best just allows issues to fester, harmful behavior to continue, and can doom both relationships and a woman's peace of mind. Don't stunt your growth by assuming that, 'he should know'."

Elliott:
"Women should exercise wisdom and patience when dealing with men - assuming that the question is about REAL MEN. There are a lot of average men, C or below, that are men impostors. Real men are A-list. Women's loneliness and need to be around a male erases patience. Then, all men begin to look the same and they can't distinguish the A-men from the C-men."

Kareem:
"What I wish women would just get about men is that we are the simplest creatures on earth and that you can take us for face value. Ain't none of us that deep. If the average man gets fed, has decent to good sex and is left alone by his spouse every now and then, he is ecstatic. Also I would like to say that the dating world would go a lot smoother if people just said what they meant and meant what they said. Can it all be so simple?"

Your Turn

Ask a man or a few men you know. Write their responses below.

Try this!

Be quiet. Listen and learn. Treasure peace.

Are you currently in a relationship? Would you like an easy way to maintain the harmony? Be quiet. There is a very good reason why.

In relationships, we need to allow more time for PEACE. Have you been accused of being a nag? Maybe you talk more than you listen. Maybe you criticize more often than necessary and you are quick to judge your man's actions without giving yourself the benefit of a peaceful moment to see what is actually going on. If you love and appreciate your man, then try to make yourself a source of peace and not stress.

Men have that macho, no-emotional-release thing going that we will never really understand. We want them to talk more; they want us to talk less. Lots of times, all they need to feel comfortable enough to share their feelings is peace and quiet.

In your peace and silence, you can find out more about your man. Suppose he's not the good man you think he is. If you'd take the time to listen to what he says and observe the things he does, you can be more in tune to what type of man he is and if he is right for you.

If you keep arguments going, criticize him at his every turn and constantly remind him that he's not so great... do you think he would want to remain committed to the relationship? Besides, if he's that much of a doofus that you have to fuss at him constantly and argue every 5 minutes... why are you with him? Move on to someone you don't have to nag. Or are you that addicted to conflict and the sound of your own voice?

Being quiet does not mean that you should not voice your opinions or speak up for yourself. It simply means that you should VALUE PEACE.

What's So Sad

Most of the people who are willing to be quiet and enjoy peace in their homes and relationships waste a lot of precious time with people who are very talkative, argumentative, critical and whiny. If you are the quiet, peaceful type, you are most likely being driven crazy by people who won't shut up. If you are the loud, argumentative or talkative type, you are most likely driving your lovers and friends crazy.

Do not use a hatchet to remove a fly from your friend's forehead. – Chinese Proverb

Know the Difference

How does your man make you feel? Like a prize or a piece of meat? Like someone whom he has to mold or someone he accepts as she is?

Positive: Your man gives you suggestions to spice up your romantic life. He may say things like:
"I think you'd look great in thigh high boots. You definitely have the legs for them."
"I'd love to see you with dark black hair. I bet that would be sexy."
"I've been dying to see you in red lacy underwear. I wouldn't be able to control myself."

These things are mere suggestions indicating that he loves you as you are but would like to keep the flame turned way up high! It's okay to take suggestions such as these in the hopes of stoking the fires of a great romance. Why not? It could be lots of fun and a way to do something a little adventurous while maintaining the intrigue and admiration of your main squeeze.

Warning: Tattoos and medical procedures are NOT fair game in attempting to maintain the spice.

Negative: Your man demeans you and criticizes your appearance. He unfairly and ruthlessly compares you to other women. He may say things like:
"My coworker had on stiletto heels today. Why don't you ever wear anything like that?"
"The girl in this video is hot. You see how flat her stomach is? Why don't you join a gym?"
"Your friend Liz has a nice haircut. You need to keep yourself up better like she does."

The Trophy

There are women who like the idea of being a man's trophy. They like the idea of being something to be shown off and held up as a prize. Women who think like this know what they want and aren't ashamed. It's a part of their femininity. Really smart women know how to play this role when the time is right. They know about men's egos and their need to brag and feel superior. Using this information to their benefit allows them much more occasion for personal amusement, courtesy of a natural difference between men and women.

Some women are totally against the idea of being a trophy, mainly because it has such as negative implication that the woman is worth nothing more than her looks. In some cases, men use women as trophies and don't put any work at all into creating a healthy relationship. They are concerned totally with their own egos while their trophy women are miserable, receiving nothing from the relationship but a quick spit-polish before being shown off again.

Positive:
In public and private, he treats you as if he is proud of you and everything about you. Not only does he speak highly of you to his friends and family, he tells you personally how great you are and how much he admires you and your traits. Your career success and demeanor merely add to physical things he finds attractive about you. When he "shows you off", you have a feeling of pride and not shame.

Negative:
He brings you around family, friends and coworkers but doesn't comment much on you as a person. You may as well be a mannequin while in public with him. He likes to brag about what you do, how you look or how much money you make as if it makes him "Da Man". In private, he criticizes you constantly, telling you that he is just trying to help you be a better person. The relationship is basically empty. All either of you gets out of it is bragging rights to your beauty and/or money.

Queen Theme: "I Can't Go For That (No Can Do)" by Hall & Oates

WORDPLAY
Your way or the high way!

It may be politically incorrect to say the following things in some circles. However, Queens of the Universe only deal with what is best for them. The following statements can certainly be true when it comes to the man you're infatuated with.

He's not good enough for you.

It has very little to do with his money, his job, his looks or anything else that a snob would tell you. It has to do with the way he treats you and if he values you and what you have to offer. You deserve nothing but the best. Settling is for peasants. Would the Queen of the Universe settle with less than she deserved? Certainly not.

You're out of his league.

Lots of undeserving men take women on guilt trips in order to get a date and/or maintain a relationship. Many women fall for these pity pleas and find themselves attached to men without jobs, money, homes or means of transportation. If a woman doesn't have all of these things for herself, then she may not be so picky. But if a woman "has it together" by her own definition, she should not give in to pressure to date a man who is not independently taking care of himself. If she wants sex, she can take it and run – why try to scrape a relationship out of it because she feels sorry for someone? Let him find a woman in his own league. Don't be a fool!

It's perfectly okay if a woman makes more than her man. The problem is when he asks you for money or expects you to support him. Let him be a man! Don't be his personal ATM. Unless you are married and he's going through a rough time in his career or is the designated home manager, you should not be giving him money. There are very few exceptions, but the most common one is if he is struggling temporarily while on his way to success. Be careful here also. He may use your money while he needs it and then drop you when he is more financially stable. Make sure that your money isn't the only reason he wants you around. Don't be a fool!

Be careful that you're not just taking on a pet project, thinking you can change a loser into a success driven, hardworking man. Be able to differentiate between a goal-oriented, upwardly mobile man and a deadbeat who doesn't do anything but daydream about what he wants to do. There is also a huge difference between a financial arrangement in a marriage and money exchanges in a boyfriend-girlfriend relationship. (See "Kings Speak" on page 142 about the difference between mothering a man and being a supportive partner.) Don't be a fool!

On the other hand, in some cases a woman is so successful in her own mind that all she really wants is a househusband who will take care of home while she is the so-called breadwinner. More power to her. Don't convince yourself or let a lazy, irresponsible man convince you that a househusband is right for you if you know that you are truly uncomfortable with such a situation. You can't trust just any man to manage household affairs and be the primary caregiver for your children. It's such an important and tough job that many women can't even do it these days. Don't be a fool!

He has nothing to offer you.
Many of the things stated above can fall under this one but there is still more. Suppose he has what you think makes a man successful and is also a nice person? He might have overwhelming child support or alimony payments that could wind up draining *your* finances while you are trying to be supportive. Maybe he has the

kind of job that consumes most of his time and he can't offer you the fact that he'd be there when you needed him.

Some men have everything in place and are all slated to be named America's next "good catch" but they lack one thing: the ability to offer you the love you deserve. Because of the way they were raised and/or their reactions to their parents' relationships, they can't relate to a woman enough to understand what makes a good relationship. A lot of these men don't even want to understand. They really can't make an emotional bond with a woman. Why should you be committed to a man who can't or won't appreciate you?

QUEEN'S RULE: THERE IS NOTHING WRONG WITH WANTING TO DEDICATE MY LIFE TO BEING A WIFE/ MOTHER/HOME MANAGER. THERE IS NOTHING WRONG WITH ME IF I *DON'T* WANT TO BE A WIFE/MOTHER/HOME MANAGER.

I can be smart when it's important but most men don't like it.
- Marilyn Monroe as Lorelei Lee in "Gentlemen Prefer Blondes" (movie)

Nobody's Business?

This is what Queen Dionne said was the best advice her mother ever gave her:

"Don't put your man around your girlfriends or talk about stuff (particularly the bad stuff) that goes on in your relationship to your girlfriends, no matter how close you and your girlfriends are."

This is what Queen Samantha submitted as her favorite quote:

"Don't listen to your friends' advice on how to keep your relationship, especially if they don't have a man."

Though many women believe these two statements, they rarely follow such advice. The key here is using your better judgment. If you have friends that you can't trust to be around your man, then they are not your friends. They are just people who are only in your life for a season and you will find that your relationship is not the only thing they will try to sabotage.

If you have true friends, you should not have a problem enjoying the company of them and your man at the same time. When you can't feel secure about your friends' and boyfriend's behavior, then you need to make changes in your life. Work on your own trust issues or trust your good judgment that either your so-called man or your so-called friends have got to go.

Contrary to what many men believe, all of a woman's friends are not after her man. Contrary to what many women believe, her man doesn't even like most of her friends, so it's unlikely that he wants to sleep with them. (However, a dog will take any sex he can get.) A good friend can get along with your man and give you support when you need her to listen to your concerns about your relationship. It doesn't matter if she has a man or not; a good friend is concerned about your happiness. Most likely, you ask her advice frequently but never take it – even if she is in a relationship. She gives you advice, knowing that you won't take it, but she is determined to be a friend to you anyway.

Every woman who is in a relationship is not qualified to give you advice. At the same time, every single woman is not single because she lacks something. She may be taking this time to be drama-free and loving every minute of it. Exercise your sense of maturity and freedom of choice when deciding what to share with friends and what not to share. Your silence can be deadly or confining you to an abusive relationship. Your silence can also deprive you of witnesses if a situation ever arises where you need to fight a legal battle. (This includes a restraining order, prosecuting a stalker or abuser, divorce or a plea of self-defense.)

You need time alone with your friends and time alone with your man. Each Queen has her own ideas of where to draw the line. The point is to not be afraid to let the two sides interact. If you have this fear, you need to dismiss your friends, your man or both.

The more time you spend on your own, with your own thoughts, enjoying your own company, the more you can figure things out for yourself. You will be more in tune with your Power Source and will intuitively know what is best for you, even if it takes you a little while to sort everything out.

Those who'll play with cats must expect to get scratched.
- Miguel DeCervantes, Spanish novelist, dramatist, poet

Trust

There is no need for a Queen of the Universe to badger her man about where he's been, when he'll call, or why he didn't call. Have some pride and dignity, why don'tcha??

If he wants you to know, he'll tell you. And if the relationship is a good and healthy one, he will tell you everything. Hopefully, you'll find yourself in a very healthy relationship in which you two feel free to tell each other everything with no hesitation, pressure, or suspicion. Relationships that involve two people who have issues with trust are doomed from the start.

Don't give him the details of your schedule unless he does the same in return. There's no need for you to be on anyone's leash. It is possible for you and your man to have a comfortable sense of freedom and maintain a loving, monogamous relationship with a strong bond of loyalty.

All men are not liars. As a matter of fact, most men think that all women are liars. However, many men are *very bad* liars. Every woman has that intuition that lets her know when something is not right in her life. You've had that feeling before; don't doubt it when you feel it again. If you think he's hiding something or can't be trusted... why do you want him around anyway? Get some dignity and a new man (or several casual acquaintances instead).

Your trust should be in the fact that your Power Source will give you all the necessary information to determine whether your relationship is right for you. Stalking is for mere mortals, not for the Queen of the Universe.

Queen Theme: "Switch" by TLC

QUEEN'S RULE: TRUST IS BEST SAVED FOR MY POWER SOURCE, NOT ANY MAN.

I'm really demanding. No girl really wants just a guy. You want a prince, you want Jesus. So when he comes around and his name is Steve, what are you supposed to do? - Macy Gray, singer

KINGS SPEAK

Question: What is the difference between mothering a man and being a supportive partner?

Roc:
"Support means encouragement. We all need it. Mothering constitutes giving him every little thing without letting him get the opportunity of enjoying the feeling as if he's getting it himself. In short, be willing to go at least halfway but allow him room to move himself. And of course, be there when he needs a shoulder."

Kato:
"Mothering a man is doing everything for him, not giving him the room to try and fend for himself. A supportive partner is a woman who does stuff with him and has his back in what he applies himself to... especially when it may even seem silly to her."

Kevin:
"I think this depends on the guy. It's in some people's nature (men and women) to nurture/protect their mate. If that's how a woman is, there's nothing wrong with that. The problem comes in if she lets her man take advantage of that. She has to be appreciated. Maybe if a woman makes her man feel smothered, he just doesn't appreciate her ways and they shouldn't be together."

Eben:
"I can't answer, but that mothering crap gets old real quick."

Shuges:
"Telling a man what to do as opposed to *suggesting* what to do."

(Remaining Anonymous):
"Easy. Doing things for him should come natural for a woman, not because she's mothering him, but because that's her man. But this is not to say that she should do everything for him. It's a two-way street. Of course he should be doing things for her as well, neither [should do things] to an excessive amount. That's when it becomes mothering or fathering. A woman should always be supportive of her man as long as it's not hurting either one of them. More often than not, it's this lack of support that causes a man to seek someone else. Hence, he's hurt from the lack of support and she's hurt from the infidelity."

Kareem :
"The difference between mothering her man and being a supportive partner is simple. Give more constructive criticism as opposed to flat out telling him what is wrong and what to do all the time. No one wants a second mother. Believe me."

Greg:
"Being a mother is [a woman saying], *You're kinda down on your luck, don't have the job you want? Let me do your resume.* If anything let ME do my resume and YOU provide assistance. Being supportive is [a woman accepting that] I can't type that well but I'm gonna use my one finger to do it myself. She can sit over my shoulder and give me guidance but not do it for me.

"Being a mother is: *I'll do that for you.* When you do it for me, what do I get from it? What do I learn? A mother is protecting me from making mistakes. Let me learn. You're wondering why [your boyfriend] doesn't step up like a man? You didn't give him the opportunity."

Elliott:
"A woman who mothers a man, in my opinion, has a high probability of being a drama queen. She's not at peace with the skin she's in. If she is at peace within, then that peace will manifest outwardly; therefore, she would be at peace with her man. As a result, she would be confident with his choices and how he handles his business... as a result, no need for mothering."

Michael James:
"Simply to let the man lead - in all matters. If the woman is letting the man lead, then she is supportive. Leading with direction, of course."

A man:
"Patience, understanding and loyalty are in the support category."

Patrick:
"Don't do anything for your man that you don't think he would do for you. Being supportive connotes a relationship where encouragement is given to allow her man to do something for himself [i.e.] encouraging words that foster a belief that he can do something for himself or is doing something valuable. The something can be broad, ranging from career goals and choices, interpersonal relationships, daily actions, or current habits.

"Encouraging acts foster the same goals but include doing things that show support, show pride, or show participation. The result allows a man to feel positive about the effort, or to add incentive through the belief that his woman is proud of the effort, or to free time to pursue the goal and foster a sense of emotional partnership.

"Whether the effort succeeds or fails, being a supportive partner allows a man to feel good about his journey. Mothering is concerned with a result or is an attempt to force a man into taking actions that he may not be ready to take. You mother a child as a part of the learning process - a disciplinary act. You support a man as part of the relationship process - a show of partnership."

WORDPLAY
Did he just say...?

The following statements are frequently made by men who are doing their very best to be honest with us about where they see the relationship going. Included is a step-by-step guide of how to take what is being said.

"I love you, but I'm not *in* love with you."

<u>Believe him.</u> Yes, you are a good catch, but don't let your ego keep you trapped when you could easily move on. (See page 156 for details.)

<u>Get away from him.</u> Maybe you can be his friend – in a year or however long it takes you to get over your disappointment. In the meantime, don't leave yourself open and vulnerable to his tendency to play with your emotions. **He will only do what you allow him to do.**

<u>Release him.</u> Why are you going through so much emotional turmoil while he is just as cool as a cucumber? All the time you spend trying to figure out how and why he said such a thing is time wasted. Will it change his mind? Will it make him cry like you have? No, it won't. Move on. It's safe. You need to make room for the new possibilities that are sure to include someone who feels just as strongly for you as you do for them.

"I don't want to get married," or "I don't EVER want to get married."

<u>Believe him.</u> Even if the truth is that he just doesn't want to marry YOU. The point is that he was honest with you. Would you rather have him discuss marriage with you

with no real intention of ever popping the question? (Happens all the time!)

Get away from him. That is, if you find your feelings growing and you think that you would like to get married. Don't let your ego tell you that you can change his mind. Next thing you know, you'll be pregnant – a subconscious way of testing a man's love when you're not married to him. (See page 95 for an eye-opener.) And suppose he does give in to your pressure (so you think). He'll do everything that a husband is not supposed to do and you'll have the nerve to wonder why. He already let you know that he wasn't marriage material.

Release him. Thank your Power Source for giving you an honest look into his future plans, or lack thereof. Wake up, Sleeping Beauty. He won't magically turn into Prince Charming and live happily ever after with you. Believe that the right person will come along, but you don't have to push it so hard. Give your Power Source the authority to make it happen. Also: Every man you meet is not potential husband material. (They can sense you holding them up to your potential husband criteria and it makes you appear undesirable and desperate.)

"I need some space."

Believe him. He may not be ready for such a serious relationship. If he's been in a serious relationship for quite some time, he may not want the serious relationship anymore. That is HIS choice, just like it would be yours if you decided that YOU needed some space. The man may be 18, 28, 38, 48 or 58 years old. He may not know what he wants but you can't force him into seeing things your way. Besides, why would you want to suffer along with him while he figures himself out? You can do badly all by yourself.

Get away from him. Hey, he said he needed space, didn't he? Just be sure you're not giving him sex while he's making up his mind. You don't have to call – not more than once a week for a quick hello. Don't accept dates more than once every two weeks and don't have sex with him. This may be his way of demoting you to a booty call. Be aware.

Release him. He'll be chasing you again soon. He expects you to keep calling and having sex with him but if you don't, his interest will intensify. Be careful. This is just his ego wanting to be sure that you are still on his roster. It doesn't mean that he is not seeing other people. Live your life. He might even say that he doesn't want the space anymore. Just make sure YOU are the one to decide when and IF you want to resume the relationship. On the other hand, he may just fade from your life. This means that, "I need some space" was his nice way to say, "I don't want to be with you anymore."

Queen Theme: "The Gambler" by Kenny Rogers

Examine what is said, not him who speaks. - Arab Proverb

I'm not in love with anybody who isn't in love with me. - Anne Shirley as Bobby Halevy in "Saturday's Children" (movie)

The Queen Takes On...
The Man Who Doesn't Spend Enough Time

Of course you should communicate EXACTLY what you would like him to do. Men need specifics. They aren't good with hints and suggestions. If he doesn't take the opportunity to pay an adequate amount of attention to a Queen as great as you are… use this handy guide. Either you'll discover that you two are not as compatible as you thought OR he'll be impressed at your ability to have a life outside of your romance and offer his time to you more freely. Remember, your relationship with him is just a part of your life, not your whole life.

DO: Get a life.

DON'T: Nag him about spending more time with you.

DO: Get a new hobby. In fact, get three.

DON'T: Feel the need to brag excessively about your activities in an attempt to get his attention.

DO: Work on your dream career.

DON'T: Treat him as if you are upset with him.

DO: FInd something that focuses your attention away from him.

DON'T: Get a hobby that keeps you in the house all the time.

DO: End the relationship if you're not getting what you want out of it.

DON'T: Become a drama queen or an attention whore. It's a turn-off and you'll lose him after all.

A romance is basically a dance, a curious back-and-forth between two people who secretly desire to have control. When one person pushes forward, the other usually draws back in some aspect of the relationship. A Queen knows how to take the lead without intimidating her man, and even knows how to keep him believing that he is the one in control when she actually is. Your goal is to keep him on the chasing end. Your tactic of stepping back doesn't have to be anything more complicated than just having a life outside of him. Keep him in pursuit of you!

If his constant attention is what you are craving, then the problem is YOU. He has a life. He'd like you to have one as well. (See page 34 on why you shouldn't rely on a man to make you happy, page 156 on how your ego causes trouble and page 43 on drama queen behavior.)

Queen Theme: "Escape (The Pina Colada Song)" by Rupert Holmes

KINGS SPEAK

The Other Woman

So you've either been cheated on, left for another woman, or able get a look at your ex-man's new woman. Often, these "other women" are not better looking, more sophisticated or more successful than we are. Men's choices in "other women" usually leave us scratching our heads and wondering about ourselves and the men we used to love.

When women cheat on or leave men, they usually upgrade for someone better looking, who has more money, more material wealth, etc. (Key word there is 'usually'.) So what's the real deal with men and their downgrading? The Focus Group Kings were BRUTALLY honest. Reader discretion is advised.

Eben:
"When I've cheated it's been with whoever wants to give up the butt when I'm ready to receive it. We men aren't financially superficial when choosing a woman to cheat with! Now when leaving a relationship (which I'd probably never do over some 'ass'), I think women just want that security of the Alpha male; it's innate. Meanwhile, the fellas would leave for that booty that's like Sunshine from the movie *Harlem Nights*…Typical animal instincts."

Greg:
"It's a control issue for men, and unfortunately in today's society, a self-esteem issue for men. If my woman is attractive, she can get any man she wants. I can't act up; I can't do the same things I can do with a woman who is less attractive. I can tell the less attractive woman, *I'm going to the moon, I'll be back.* You can't tell the woman

who has it all that you're going to the moon. She'll say, *I won't be here when you get back.*

"If I'm with this woman, I know that at any point she can leave me for another man. If I'm with a woman who is not as good, I can treat her in any way. I can talk to her in any way. She believes that I'm the best she's ever gonna have. But a woman who is very attractive, a woman who does well for herself financially... If she's not happy, she can always leave. A lot of guys are with certain females because the women will let them do whatever.

"Men were raised to be the sole provider and have their wives dependent on them. These days, our wives are making more money. I'm not the provider. I can't buy her a bunch of things. As a matter of fact, she may be buying me things. Men these days have to take on a role of emotional supporter. We have to learn how to support our wives and take care of our families. Women today with this newfound freedom and money have to understand that even though they are making more money, they have to understand their role in the family. They don't put trust in their mates."

Elliott:
"[Some men are] ignorant and self-conscious about their own inaccuracies. [They have] low self-esteem, low self-confidence, they need to be mothered by their mates and they pretty much match perfectly with drama queens!"

Shuges:
"The power of the p-u-s-s-y. If it's flung at a man, chances are, he's gonna try and hit it whereas a woman will (over)analyze the situation a bit more. Dudes are less likely to get emotionally involved or even look at things from that perspective. He'll say, *Awww shit, she wants some dick,* and he'll start pressing and making advances for some play. Meanwhile, the chick is like, *I wanna fuck him, BUT...*

There's always a 'but'. In other words, females almost all the time have to like the guy beyond the physical aspect of things. The guy just has to like her ass, her tits, the way she walks, her smell, the way she dresses, her hair, her lips, her legs, etc, etc, etc. Also, chicks who can't rely on their looks usually score high in other areas. She'll give a man attention and the next thing you know, he's down to dig her out."

Kato:
"[Men downgrading] is not always the case. And during the times when that is the case, it's mainly just the pussy on the brain... unless the less attractive or chicken-head types are more of a supportive partner instead of a mother."

Kevin:
"I think women like to feel complimented and women care about how they're treated. Men like to feel needed. So if I'm right, in the long term, a woman looks for someone who is her equal (or complement), but she'll leave that guy for somebody better (or someone who TREATS her better than the guy she was with before). A man wants to find his complement, but after a while, he doesn't feel as needed as he once did. That's when he starts spending more time with someone he feels needs him more than the woman he has."

DeLano:
"It is obvious that when people cheat, they cheat because there is something that they aren't getting at home. They are bored, the spice is gone, the things you used to do you don't do anymore, etc, etc. For men, easy is better!! Those chicken-heads/crack-heads/hoochies/tramps/skeezas are much easier to get into bed and into some position that your CEO/President/Partner woman won't. You don't have to buy them dinner or take them to the theater.

They are fairly low maintenance (you can always find them and they have no meetings to attend). They don't belong to any civic organizations [nor do they] do any community service to keep them from catering to the man and unlike the relationship at home, the MAN is in total control. Well, most of the time.

"I think women go for the Power Guy or the Renaissance Man. The Power Guy flies you to islands for the weekend, [takes you to] 5 star hotels, [gives you] strawberries and cream with the Dom Perignon or whatever. The Renaissance Man reads to you, rubs your feet, paints your portrait, writes you poems and songs and plays a mean acoustic guitar! Those dudes get on my nerves. (I am taking art and guitar lessons as we speak.) Anyway, I digress.

"I guess if you want to keep you partner at home, keep on doing what you did to get him or her. Don't be afraid to try new things, go places, travel, read a book together, rub [his/her] back, cook her dinner even if it is grilled cheese and soup - my specialty, take her to a game, take him to the spa, share your passions, dreams, goals, etc."

Slick:
"SEX!"

Michael James:
"Women usually cheat on the emotional level, someone who is listening to them and being attentive, so they will sleep with anyone who provides that - CEO or burger flipper. Deep down, many women want to be taken care of. They want the man to be in charge. Period. And to be in charge the man has to make more money so he can keep her in check (not his thinking but hers, feeling that, *Well he does provide this and that; I should listen to him.*)

"Women also have been fed a fairly tale life from the media (television, books, movies) so they unconsciously want to sit back and let the man take care of them. Of course they can make their own money and have a career, but they want that as an option, not a must.

"Men - it's very simple. Men just want respect and to wear the pants. We want to enjoy life without drama and keeping up with the Joneses. Our egos are huge, so it is better to find someone whom we can co-exist with. Their pockets are never a subject of our lust or love. We are very simple. Respect us and you are the one. Period."

Roc:
"New girl is doing something that old girl isn't."

Women need a reason to have sex. Men just need a place.
- Billy Crystal, actor and comedian

Mirror, Mirror

How our ego trips can drive us crazy and
keep us stalled in dysfunctional relationships
with the wrong men

Do you know this woman? She's pretty, smart, has a good job, is independent, and seems to have it all. Men flock to her and she enjoys their attention. The problem is: she gets into relationships with men who treat her as if she's no different than any other woman on the street. Of course, the relationships don't begin that way...

Every once in a while she gives into one of her pursuers and he tells her how wonderful and beautiful she is, just as the others do. *Something* about him makes her guards come down and she soon finds herself in a serious relationship with a man who seems intent on having her as his own. That *something* about him makes her "fall in love" (she thinks), but time goes by and he changes (she thinks). After the relationship continues at a serious pace for a while, she notices that he isn't as attentive as he used to be. He doesn't give her the most basic of common courtesies such as a phone call to say his plans have changed, asking her opinion on something of importance, or simply coming home before dawn.

Their arguing becomes more frequent and usually, in time, she becomes a drama queen (if only in the confines of the relationship). He does things to hurt her deliberately, though he claims them to be unintentional. No matter how much she cries, fusses or makes scenes in order to make him see how hurt she is... he keeps his disrespectful habits. Sometimes she gets fed up and threatens to leave. He agrees at first but changes his mind when it looks as if she's serious, then he makes up with her. She stays, thinking that he will change, and things go well until he does the same things again. The cycle continues. Do you know this woman?

Why does he do this to her?
He actually wants to break up with her but can't bring himself to end it. He'd rather keep pushing her buttons until *she* breaks it off. He also starts to count on the fact that no matter what he does to her, she will stay with him. He doesn't care about her pain, crying or drama. He only knows that she STAYS and puts up with him. Why should he change?

If she has so much going for her, why wouldn't he want to settle down and be with her?
First of all, she starts to require way too much of his attention. Second, her novelty has worn off. Sure, he likes knowing that he has a pretty, smart, independent woman but that is just to appease his ego. He was happy to give her all the attention she craved in the beginning. After all, he had something to gain: her sex and eventually, her heart. Once his mission was accomplished, he had nothing to work for – especially if he found that he could do whatever he wanted and all she'd do is cry or fuss. She wants attention, attention and more attention. This is how her ego messes it up. He is, in effect, turned off by her need to feed her ego with his attention.

In many cases, he felt that she was too good for him in the first place. But, a man's way is to conquer; he'll do it whenever possible and without thinking too much about it. Eventually, he may want to leave the relationship for a woman who doesn't have it all; that way, he can feel as if HE is the prize - not his constant attention. (See previous "Kings Speak" on page 151.)

If she were to be serious about leaving him, why would he ask her to stay?

She has become a habit to him, even if he doesn't realize it. He has become used to her and the different things she does to try and keep his attention. These things range from housekeeping to sexual favors to playing second mom to his kids. Also, it makes him look good to have such a woman as his main squeeze – no matter how many women he may have on the side. Despite her drama, she's still a trophy.

He hasn't made up his mind about what he wants in life and doesn't see the harm in dragging her along in his aimless confusion. In many of these cases, he has willingly discussed marriage and children with her. She has gotten her hopes up about something that he wasn't serious about. There are cases when a man discusses marriage and kids for the sole purpose of keeping a woman hanging on, knowing full well that he doesn't intend to spend his life with her.

If he does so many deceitful things, why is it HER ego that's the problem?

He will only do what she *allows* him to do. Remember, she's the woman who has it all. Men's worship and other women's envy have gone to her head. She is used to getting tons of attention and completely falls apart when she doesn't get it. The ego-driven woman may tell her friends, "I can do better than him," but her ego gets in the way of actually moving on to find something better.

When a man doesn't give her the attention she is used to, he becomes a challenge to her. That's that *something* she sensed in the very beginning that drew her to him in the first place. When things go wrong, it won't occur to her to break up with him. She will simply keep vying for his attention. There are times when the dishonesty and disrespect are totally obvious, but her ego refuses to accept that this man doesn't want her.

It's basically subconscious, of course. After time, it's not the man she wants; it's his attention. Her ego keeps her from seeing the fool she makes of herself again and again until it's too late. It takes 100 or more crying episodes in addition to the man doing something really horrible in order for her to leave. She winds up emotionally devastated but finds herself in a similar situation with the next relationship.

What's a Queen to do?
Being Queen of the Universe is not how great you think you are, but how great you believe your Power Source is. Queens of the Universe don't seek attention, nor do they thrive on it. They thrive solely on the mercy and miracles of their Power Source. All other positives just fall into line. Queens of the Universe rely on that all-knowing voice inside to tell them, "when to hold them, when to fold them, when to walk away, and when to run." Especially in romantic relationships.

One day, he gon' say, 'You crowdin' my space.' – Erykah Badu, from "Bag Lady" (song)

The Queen Takes On...
The Cheating Lover

DO: Leave him permanently or temporarily until you are thinking more clearly.

DON'T: Stay with him. A distance is necessary because you both need to think about the relationship.

DO: Thank your Power Source for revealing the truth so that you could make an informed decision about your relationship.

DON'T: Let your ego get in the way and try to fight for him. Why would you want a cheater?

DO: Release him and his inability to be monogamous.

DON'T: Blame the other woman. He had an obligation to you; she didn't (unless she's a close friend of yours). In that case, release them both.

DO: Expect him to take responsibility for what he did or is doing.

DON'T: Beat yourself up about it or allow yourself to be conned into thinking that it is your fault.

DO: Carry yourself as the Queen of the Universe.

DON'T: Carry yourself as a scorned woman.

DO: Keep your dignity, self-respect and trust in your Power Source.

DON'T: Stalk, harm or harass the other woman. She already has the short end of the stick - that no good man to deal with.

DO: Stay away from the other woman and don't talk to her

DON'T: Consider yourself threatening her or even warning her about how much of a dog the man is. If she wants him, she'll keep seeing him.

You're going to need some theme music for this one. Note to Queen: Don't do anything violent after singing aloud to "Caught Out There" by Kelis. (See page 209 for more examples. Also see page 170 for why you shouldn't be listening to sappy love songs while you are attempting to move on.)

Don't cry for a man who's left you; the next one may fall for your smile. – Mae West, actress

Know the Difference

There is a difference between staying with someone out of a false sense of obligation and staying with someone because there is truly a foundation for a meaningful relationship. The foundation of a strong, good, healthy relationship is not built on sex, money, attention, a few laughs, a child, or time spent in the relationship. If any one of these things is your excuse to stay in a relationship and you're not happy, then it's time to free yourself. The foundation of a good, strong, healthy relationship fit for a Queen and King is planted much deeper than those things that are so easily found.

Some unhealthy reasons why some Queens stay:

Family Expectations

A lot of Queens have well-meaning family members who want the best for them. A love life is no exception. However, the well-meaning family members may push a Queen to stay in a relationship where she is not happy. They aren't thinking of your idea of happiness. They are forcing you to accept their ideas of happiness and their need for keeping up appearances – even if they aren't doing it maliciously. Keep in mind that YOU are the person who is in the relationship, not them. Appreciate the fact that your family cares so much, but believe that you deserve to be happy.

Friends' Opinions

A Queen's friends also have to remember that SHE is the one in the relationship, not them. Especially in her youth, a Queen's friends can pressure her to be in a relationship for the wrong reasons. The reasons vary from social status to money to mere physical attraction. If your friends value materialism over your divine right to be happy, you need to distance yourself from them. No need to cut them totally off, but if you are spending your life trying to keep up with their empty values you will never feel "good enough" just as you are.

Bad Habit
A man can be just as bad a habit as smoking, biting your nails, or overeating. In some relationships, a Queen's partner is simply a compulsive behavior that results from a deep-rooted problem or issue that has yet to be resolved in her consciousness. One dictionary defines a habit as: 1. A continual, often involuntary or unconscious inclination to perform an activity, acquired through frequent repetition. 2. An addiction. 3. An activity done without thinking.

Wow. Some Queens stay in bad relationships *involuntarily, unconsciously, addictively,* and *without thinking.*

Unconscious? Not thinking? It's time to wake up!! Why is a habit deemed bad only when physical destruction is apparent? What about mental and emotional destruction? Many Queens have been through this and some still have yet to go through it. Cutesy, romantic songs throughout the ages even seem to imply that it's just "love" that keeps you "addicted" to him and not able to stay away. (See page 170 for information on how love songs can screw with our minds.)

See that first definition for a habit. It is an inclination acquired through frequent repetition. That means, you have been with the person for so long, you just get used to being with them – even if the relationship is a bad one. If someone you loved was on crack for years and told you that they weren't going to stop because they had invested too much time into the relationship with the pipe... Okay, it's even too stupid of an idea to finish. If your man is your crack pipe, it's time for rehab.

Time

It doesn't matter how long you have been in a relationship. It can take anywhere from two weeks to over 20 years for your relationship to fall apart. You may feel as if you've "invested" so much time into a relationship – but what did you really expect to get in return? A free pass into heaven? Come on! Maybe you expected a crapload of money. If that's the case, you were in it for the wrong reasons anyway.

Time is but a concept and there are people all over the world who believe that there is no such thing. Time does not make a good relationship nor does it give a good reason to stay. If anything, you should look at the time spent in the bad relationship and say, "I've spent too much time taking this crap! It's time for me to have a good life!"

Time makes lovers feel like they've got something real.
- Culture Club, "Time (Clock of the Heart)" (song)

Finances

This is only a small part of why the Women's Rights Movement started - so Queens could be able to make their own money and take care of their families if they had to. Even if you think you lack the proper skills, education, and training, there are programs in your state set up especially for women like you to find good jobs. Even if you don't want to attempt a traditional form of employment, you have certain natural skills and abilities that will allow you to make money and support yourself.

Some Queens already have jobs and are making their own money but still feel that they need their mate's salary to survive. Maybe they've become "accustomed" to a certain way of living. Bull. The basics are: food, clothing and shelter. Transportation can be added in some cases. The basics are not: an expensive car, a very big house, designer clothing, and junk food. We enjoy many luxuries that are simply not necessary. It's no crime to enjoy them if we can afford them – many of us work damn hard for our money – but if you need to forsake a few material things in order to leave a bad relationship and/or bring your kids up in a safe environment, make a sacrifice.

Material Gain

It doesn't matter who he is, what he does for a living or how much money and presents he gives you. If all you're getting out of a relationship is money, how can you be happy with it? (Unless you've got someone on the side.) All that glitters isn't gold and it will blind you if you're not careful. You think you're getting over on him but you're only cheating yourself. Don't you deserve more? If you can't give up the addiction of the glamorous life, then you don't think much of yourself. It's all an illusion that can be taken away from you in the blink of an eye – such as when he decides he doesn't want to share it with you any longer. He's already got your replacement waiting.

Sympathy

Some people will play the sympathy card every time you try to end it and use your guilt to trap you into a relationship. Maybe he does love you, but more than that, he wants your sympathy. Life is work enough for a Queen without shouldering the burdens of a man who refuses to grow up and get his life together or end a cycle of pain in his life. Sure, you can be his friend if it's feasible. However, he has a responsibility to himself and his Power Source to prioritize his drama over his sexual desire and loneliness. Allow him to be a man and work out his own issues before you continue into an abyss of "helping a guy when he's down".

Kings Speak:
"That sympathy turns into misery for the person who's being sympathetic." – Rico
"You feel sorry for him but who's feeling sorry for you?" – Lou

Marriage
Don't use the empty-yet-pious-sounding excuse of, "I promised before God to be with this man until death." If you're in a horrible marriage, do you think that God wants you to be miserable until death? Everything that you do, you do 'before God' and God knew when you uttered those words that it wasn't a match made in heaven. God teaches us lessons when we ignore the warning signs that are shown to us. More likely than not, you saw warnings before you walked down the aisle but you ignored them. Swear you didn't see any of these bad days coming? Well, you see them now. Don't let "Til death do us part" mean until he kills you or you kill him. Even if the marriage is not physically abusive, you know when someone is treating you badly. Say your prayers and do what you feel is necessary.

Loneliness
Some women are only in relationships because they are afraid of being alone or lonely. They have actually never given themselves the chance to experience real love that only comes from their Power Source. They have never learned how to be their own friends and lovers. A man's physical presence does not guarantee the emotional support you are seeking.

Low Self-Esteem

Do you know that some men prey on women with low self-esteem? They purposely find a woman who thinks so little of herself that she will accept anything he does and says to her. Some men find women with high self-esteem and make it their business to destroy the women's sense of self-worth through emotional, verbal and mental abuse in order to make them more subservient.

Emotional and verbal abuse keeps many women trapped. Some of us have issues stemming from childhood abuse and we aren't aware that we are lost in that cycle. Therefore, we don't realize that we deserve much better than what we are getting from the men we choose. Some of us got into relationships with men whom we thought we could change, and instead, they changed us. They made us believe that we thought too highly of ourselves and once our self-esteem was shattered, we let them do almost anything to us. Hopefully, this book will lend a hand to those Queens who need a push in the right direction - up to their Universal Thrones.

Sex
Many women get married just so they can have sex without feeling like they are committing a sin against their religion. If you are *that* religious, then trust your Higher Power to bring you the right person at the right time and to control your urges while you wait.

Losing him does not matter. It is you who will be found... and cherished. - France Nuyen as Ying-Ying St. Clair in "The Joy Luck Club" (movie)

WORDPLAY
Sorry, I can't stay...

These statements have been held in high regard for centuries. However, when it comes to a Queen's romantic relationships, she should not take them as absolute gospel. Trust your gut feeling and don't let the following advice from others keep you in a bad situation.

Running away won't solve anything.
According to one of the Queen of the Universe theme songs, "The Gambler", we need to know when to walk away and when to run. Running away from an abusive or potentially harmful relationship doesn't mean that you are weak. It means you are smart - even if you're married. Being smart enough to run away could save your life. Be careful not to run straight into the same situation with a different person because you didn't give yourself time to release the pain of the previous situation.

Don't leave at the first sign of trouble.
Define trouble. Did he leave his socks on the floor or did he harm your child? Did he leave the toilet seat up or did he expose you to something illegal that could get you into trouble? Did he invite his friends over and leave you to clean up the mess or did you catch him with another woman? Some issues are easily worked out between two people in a healthy, loving relationship while others signal very serious problems.

Did he abuse you emotionally, verbally, or mentally? Those forms of abuse hurt just as bad as the physical and it only gets worse as time goes on – no matter how many times he apologizes and buys off your pain. Fool you once, shame on him. Fool you twice, shame on YOU. You know deep down inside when you are not comfortable with a situation. Staying in a potentially abusive, troublesome or deadly relationship serves absolutely no one.

Don't let a religious institution or well-meaning family member guilt-trip you into "working it out" when you know that you are in danger. You are the one in the relationship – not the people telling you to work it out. Besides, it takes both parties in the relationship to work it out. You'll drive yourself crazy trying to "work it out" with someone who does not respect you or the relationship. Take responsibility for your life. Leave at the first sign of trouble. Report to the authorities if the situation warrants.

We are shown many warning signs in the beginning of a relationship, but infatuation, loneliness and low self-esteem cause us to overlook these things. Keep your eyes open, your mind alert and your heart faithful to your Power Source.

Forgive and forget.
This is often taken out of context and can be used to keep a person stuck in doormat mode. Forgiving him for something does not mean that you have to stay with him. You can forgive him, then forget HIM. Don't forget what happened to you or how it made you feel. Remember the lesson you learned so that you won't find yourself taking the same crap again in the next relationship.

The way most people go about it, they use more brains picking a horse in the third at Belmont than they do picking a husband.
– Lauren Bacall as Ms. Page in "How to Marry a Millionaire" (movie)

Mirror, Mirror

Why your preferred forms of entertainment may be locking you into a series of bad relationships.

Songs written for men vary from misogynistic to cynical, from violent to funny. Unfortunately, popular songs written for a female audience usually have a lovesick or male-bashing tone. There are distinct differences between men and women, causing each side to hopelessly seek understanding from the other. The relentless pursuit of common ground usually ends in disappointment and resentment because neither side has ceased to allow itself to be conditioned by the entertainment industry - the great divider.

It seems that only the stuffiest, most judgmental censorship advocates believe that music can affect our thoughts and actions. Though their methods and reasons may seem a little insane, the more open-minded of us can take a little nudge from them and at least examine the music we listen to and consider how it affects our lives.

As Queens of the Universe, our leadership roles require that we give notice to all aspects of our lives - including what we regard as "entertainment only". When we listen to so-called love songs, we are usually listening to women profess the following feelings:

-How she would do anything - even die - for her man

-How she is so insanely in love with her man (This is actually called obsession, which leads to stalking and restraining orders.)

-How her man dogged her, but his "lovin'" is so good

that she can't stay away from him

-How her family and friends warned her that her man was no good but he makes her feel like no one else ever has (low self-esteem alert!)

-How some other woman is trying to steal her man but he is all hers and she won't let him go

      This is all way too pathetic for the Queen of the Universe.

      Even most of the love songs written by men include tons of romantic, superman claims that 99% of women will never experience from a man. Every woman *could* experience such romantic luxury with a man, but the majority of women find that the men offering such chivalry and worship are not their types. Instead, these women pick the tough guy types and convince themselves that they can change Mr. Caveman into Mr. Sensitive.

How do men feel about these songs, books, and movies that are geared toward women?
      Think of the books, songs and movies about sweet, romantic men who sweep women off their feet and do all those things that make us say, "Awwww..." That's why these things are called "chick flicks," etc. Most men reject that view of a sweet, overly romantic man whose sole aim in life is pleasing his woman. There are some men who don't mind getting overly romantic (very often) for their women, but most women find those men sexually unattractive.

      The majority of men like to maintain their strong tough guy images, complete with an obsession with violence, a love of danger, and lust for many women. Even if they aren't prone to criminal behavior, senseless violence or infidelity, society dictates that they have to project a certain image in order to be considered "real men". That is why the songs, books, and movies men write for male audiences have themes of misogyny, violence and crude humor. It's one of the things that separate the male gender from the female gender.

We have to accept this and deal with it accordingly. From birth, men and women are expected to behave certain ways and think certain thoughts. It's why most fathers are extremely opposed to boys playing with dolls or exploring their mother's closets. These gender expectations form our behaviors throughout life.

If there are men who will do and say the things in chick flicks, love songs, and romance novels, why do women find them unattractive?
Most women like "bad boys". This doesn't mean that all women are attracted to inmates, drug abusers or domestic abusers, but the average woman wants to feel protected by a man whom she perceives as stronger, smarter and/or tougher than herself. Part of it is just the human tendency of loving a challenge and valuing certain traits in a mate that are completely different from one's own. Women, as much as we hate to admit it, like the thrill of trying to tame a man or change him into a better person somehow. As she grows older, a woman evolves regarding what she thinks she can change about men. In youth, she may have believed she could make a man faithful and romantic. In her maturity, she may believe that she can make a man eat more salads.

Many times, Mr. Sensitive is constantly passed up because he appears far too willing to do all of the romantic things described in songs or acted out on film. Women often get the impression that he is only willing to do those things in order to compensate for something else he lacks. If he is insecure about his physical appearance, a low-paying job or something else that he feels makes women run from him, women pick up on this and react accordingly. A man's lack of qualities that women find attractive may be a figment of his own imagination, stemming from deep-rooted insecurity and poor self-esteem. Of course, any insecure person drives lovers away. Insecurity in a man makes him look and act like he is weak. Women pass him up for someone with a tough streak who makes them feel protected and somewhat challenged. The problem is that they expect the tough guys to behave like the sensitive men they pass up. It's insanity.

Women do not like timid men. Cats do not like prudent rats. - H.L. Mencken, American writer and critic of American life

What's a Queen to do?
Draw the line between entertainment and real life. Most of us are smart enough to separate the two until we are in a relationship that we are not sure if we should get out of. Then, while we're listening to the radio or a favorite CD, trying to focus on keeping a shred of dignity... a love song comes on. The woman singing seems to be narrating our exact situation and by the end of the song, she's back with the man whom she was trying to break up with. *Because his love is so good.* Whatever. We internalize the lyrics and justify our unhealthy relationship, then stay with the man. We let him keep hurting us because we've come to the conclusion that love is supposed to hurt. After all, that's what the love songs say.

Stop being a hopeless romantic. It increases your chances of being used by men. Some women find the hopeless romantic trait to be cute and feminine, but the men whom those women are attracted to find it annoying and unattractive. The only purpose that a hopeless romantic can serve to a "bad boy" is being a doormat, ATM or punching bag because he knows that her head is so far up into the clouds, he can do anything to her and she'll justify it because he's her man. The hopeless romantic women are guilty of the same things that the sensitive, romantic men are guilty of. They are more likely to pursue someone who is a challenge instead of pursuing someone who will genuinely appreciate their generous ways.

Beware of the gigolos. There are attractive, confident men who use excessive romance in order to prey on women displaying a low sense of self-worth or other desperate vibes. They often obtain money, services or a place to live from different women at different times. Many wear the Mr. Romance mask just to get sex and it feeds their egos tremendously.

Accept a man for all of his bad boy/caveman faults OR give one of the insecure, boring, way-too-nice guys a chance to love you. You are driving your man nuts by expecting him to get as mushy as a fictional character in a song, book or movie. Men show their love in very different ways than women do. They also have their own paces for expressing their feelings. Keep in mind that all men think that they are romantic in a sense. A particular man's idea of what is romantic will satisfy some women and totally outrage others. But, it is up to him to find the woman with whom he is most compatible, just as it is your responsibility to find whose special brand of romance works for you. So many women latch onto a guy for his "bad boy" traits and then hound him about not being more sensitive and romantic. Why do they expect these men to change? That's like them expecting us to start obsessing over sports, working under the hood of the car just for the heck of it, farting and burping for public fun, or getting a subscription to a nudie magazine because we really love the pictures.

Stop fantasizing and appreciate the man. He is not a character; he is real. Don't continue to begin relationships only seeing what you want to see or planning what you would like to change about him. Men tell us and show us all we need to know about them within the first few dates. Women choose to overlook these flashing neon signs because we are thinking that this may be the guy we've been fantasizing about. Just to satisfy our quest for the perfect men and relationships, we dismiss the warning signs as something that we might change or tolerate. Later in the relationship when time has allowed the fog to clear, we wonder why they changed so much. Guess what? They didn't change. Those traits have been there all along, but we were too deep into a fantasy.

Don't equate good sex with a good relationship. You want a "piece" or do you want "peace"? Are you staying because his *love* is so good to you or because his *sex* is so good to you?

Pay attention to more of men's entertainment. It projects a lot of things about women that we regard as ignorant, gross, dysfunctional and misogynistic. But, if this is what guys are listening to, absorbing and discussing about women... don't you think you need to pay attention? It is up to you to use this information to your own benefit. Open your mind and fill that mental file marked "men" by using your mind and not your heart (for once).

You know how it is when you get those, uh, manly urges and you just have to kill something... fix things, uh, cook outdoors...
– Mulan, "Mulan" (movie)

The Queen Takes On... The Ex

DO: Remember the good times and think of how your new lover will give you even better ones.

DON'T: Dwell on the times they hurt you. That just allows them to hurt you all over again.

DO: Remember phrases like, "What goes around comes around," and "Karma is a mother..."

DON'T: Intentionally seek revenge with threats, bodily harm or destruction of property. It's tough, but are they worth possibly going to jail for? Hell no!

DO: Turn feelings of jealousy into pity for your ex's new girlfriend. She's really in for it, the poor thing.

DON'T: Threaten the new girlfriend. A civil, but firm conversation may be needed if she will be around your kids.

DO: Keep venting to a minimum. Ask your friends to tell you to stop when you say the ex's name. Have an All Hail the Queen Jamboree instead! (see page 53)

DON'T: Constantly talk about the ex to your friends and family. They'll start to avoid you. A few weeks vent time should be sufficient.

DO: Limit all conversation with the ex to once a month (or even less). Show him that you're the Queen and that he lost out. Action speaks louder than words. If you're not always there to answer the phone, the door, or his emails, he'll know you have a life.

DON'T: Spend too much time in conversation with the ex, rehashing the gory details of the break-up. It's also not necessary to make up stories of how good or bad you're doing without him.

DO: Seek lessons from the experience so that you will never allow anyone else to hurt you in that way.

DON'T: Put up a shield and deny any new relationships that may blossom. It is possible to learn a lesson and move on happily.

DO: Be thankful for the time you will spend without him. It can be used constructively.

DON'T: Waste time by crying and stressing over the situation. .

DO: Take time to enjoy the single life.

DON'T: Be in a hurry to get into another relationship.

Men are like buses and trains. If you miss one, you will catch another one. – Rebecca's Granny (submitted by Rebecca, a Focus Group Queen)

Whatcha Really Want

So, there's a man you THINK you want. A coworker, a neighbor, a stranger, a fellow club-hopper... perhaps the one who sleeps in your bed every night?

Has there ever been a time when you wanted someone so badly... then wound up wanting to get rid of him quickly when you actually got him? Don't beat yourself up, Queen. That's what we call a lesson learned. It is so possible, so necessary to leave all things up to your Power Source – even Love.

You can do all of the things a man likes (according to our Focus Group Kings) such as give him regular sex, kinky sex, home-cooked meals, time to himself and a strong sense of support, but that will not make him change into the man you want him to be. Your goal here is to find the person who is the most compatible with you and willing to give you the respect that you deserve. The Queen of the Universe deserves nothing less than the most worthy partner.

Ask Divine Wisdom NOT for that person you *think* you want, but for the right person for you. Ask Divine Wisdom NOT to change the man you want, but to change you.

Keep in Mind

People enter into relationships that serve some sort of purpose for them. Moreover, each woman has her own set of "issues" that she can deal with in a relationship and no two women are exactly alike.

Some women can deal with a messy man as long as he doesn't talk much. Some women can deal with a man with no money as long as he is faithful. Some women don't mind infidelity as long as the man provides for her financially. This is just a short list of many issues on which women differ when it comes to their relationships.

What goes on between two people infatuated is usually something that no one else can fully understand. However, don't let a man use that fact to keep you in a dysfunctional relationship when he notices that your family and friends are trying to help you realize that you are being disrespected by him.

Your relationship is up to you, but do not settle for less than you deserve!

Gotta Get Away?

If you're coming into a healthy sense of self-worth, gaining self-esteem by the second, and displaying overall Queen of the Universe qualities... The man you were with and/or the men trying to become a part of your life are going to go temporarily crazy. They aren't used to the Queen and her spiritual level of confidence. They are used to having it *their* way. It's up to you to draw the line and make cut-backs where needed.

Entering into a new awareness of Life and Love will make you see your relationship in terms of what you feel that you deserve. Consequently, you might find yourself gathering the strength to leave a man who is not in your best interest. Beware: The man you're trying to get away from will do whatever he can to hold on to you. However, this doesn't mean that you should *let* him hold on.

He may compliment you...

He may beg you...
He may tell you that you're the only woman for him...
He may try to give you guilt trips...
He may throw temper tantrums...
He may cry...
He may threaten you...
He may even change his ways temporarily.

    All of the tactics he'll use are tests to see what will work to keep you. He doesn't know if the begging, the guilt, or any emotional displays will get a reaction in his favor. He doesn't know until you fall for it. And even if you do... It doesn't mean that he'll treat you better or love you more. It means you stayed with him. That's it. That's all you get out of it - more of his bullcrap. He, on the other hand, gets YOU. You're the prize, the Queen of the Universe. He isn't a prize at all, which is why you wanted to leave in the first place. And as soon as he is comfortable, he will go back to his old self. Except, things will get worse.

Remember: They must come UP to your level. You must not go DOWN to theirs.

Got Away

If you are going through a breakup or are still stressing over your last one, don't play the blame game. **He only did what you allowed him to do.** No need to beat yourself up about it, though. Let him go and all of his baggage as well. Take the dead weight from around your neck and breathe. This is your opportunity to be free – to get to know yourself and make a stronger connection with your Power Source. You weren't born into this world connected to him so when it all boils down, he's just a habit you've acquired over some time. Pray for strength and break it!

Pass Up the Rebound

Be careful with "Rebound Man" or "Transition Guy". Women may want to go to either of the two soon after her relationship ends. Rebounds come with what seems to be serious emotional involvement, but Transition Guys are strictly for entertainment and only meant to ease the transition from Lockdown into Single City. If you get involved with someone else too quickly, you run the risk of bringing in issues left over from the relationship you are trying to get over. Don't put yourself or a new guy through unnecessary stress when a little time alone is what you really need.

For the Queens who've made it out of a bad relationship:

Whatchu gonna do when you get outta jail? I'm gonna have some fun! - Tom Tom Club, "Genius of Love" (song)

For you Queens who would still like to "settle down" with "the right man" at some point:

It took so long... still I believed... somehow the one that I needed would find me eventually. - Mariah Carey, "Vision of Love" (song)

For you Queens who are using your brains and not your hearts:

If you want to sacrifice the admiration of many men for the criticism of one, go ahead, get married. - Katharine Hepburn, actress and writer

For the Queens who think they'll miss the sex:

Your penis is kind of nice. Too bad you're attached to it.
- Mena Suvari as Edie in "Six Feet Under" (HBO)

HIStory

Take a look at what men from all over the world have said about women throughout the ages. You may be amused, shocked or pleasantly surprised by what you are about to read. Whatever your feelings on these sentiments, be sure to keep them in mind and use the information wisely.

"Man has his will – but woman has her way." – Oliver Wendell Holmes, American poet, essayist and physician, from *The Autocrat of the Breakfast Table*

"Women are meant to be loved, not to be understood." – Oscar Wilde, Irish writer and playwright

"A man who has never made a woman angry is a failure in life." – Christopher Morley, American writer and Rhodes Scholar

"In revenge and in love, woman is more barbarous than man." – Friedrich Nietzsche, German 'philosopher'

"The great living experience for every man is his adventure into the woman. The man embraces in the woman all that is not himself, and from that one resultant, from that embrace, comes every new action." – D.H. Lawrence, British author

"I should like to know what is the proper function of women, if it is not to make reasons for husbands to stay at home, and still stronger reasons for bachelors to go out." – George Eliot, British novelist

"I must have women. There is nothing that unbends the mind like them." – John Gay, British playwright, poet

"Women cannot complain about men anymore until they start getting better taste in them." - Bill Maher, comedian and television personality

"There are only two types of women – goddesses and doormats." – Pablo Picasso, Spanish artist

KINGS SPEAK

Question: Think of a woman who is closest to your idea of perfection. What is it about her that makes her so great?

Roc:
"She's like having a sister around. Sometimes I forget she's a girl. Perfect girl: Brother/ sister/ Mom/ Dad/ cousin/ girlfriend/ pastor/ therapist."

Eben:
"I dunno."

Dave:
"Attitude, intelligence and the love for herself, mentally and physically, makes her pure and worthy."

Greg:
"She was compassionate, athletic, caring, had a wonderful personality, and was intellectual, supportive, and able to communicate." *[Greg was asked why he didn't pursue a long-term relationship with her.]* "I was 21 years old and I thought I was missing out on the world."

Kareem:
"The woman I am thinking of whom I consider perfect has a very good blend of five qualities; Independence, class, personality, empathy and spirituality. By the way, she is just as sweet a person as she is beautiful physically."

Shuges:
"For me it's pretty simple. A woman who's nice - and I mean genuinely nice - or one who cares is already ahead

of the pack because it's so hard (for me at least) to be an asshole to someone who isn't acting like one towards me. Physical appearance isn't really as high on the list as most women may think. Why do you think guys fuck around with so many busted chicks? 1 part sweet + 1 part supportive + 1 part sexy - 1 part trashy - 1 part nagging + 1 part independent = a pretty good start to perfection."

Kevin:
"I don't know... I never know... I think that's my problem... I don't know what to look for..."

Patrick:
"She pays attention-to herself and to others. She has enough trust in herself to be an equal partner in romantic, social, and professional relationships. This means that she isn't afraid to assert her needs, be honest in her opinions, and take steps that allow her to grow.

"Additionally, she has a good heart. This means that she isn't afraid of giving of herself to others. She listens instead of waiting for her turn to speak. She makes a real effort to make others feel appreciated for their efforts or interest...even when this isn't convenient for her and even when those efforts or interests are directed at her. She knows that she has flaws, but acknowledges them and takes time to make them better.

"She assumes that others have a good character, and even when proven wrong she doesn't let that affect her treatment of others. All this and she's beautiful! Essentially her identity and independence cultivate a unique set of experiences that enrich those close to her, and her caring nature results in countless selfless acts that allow others to enrich themselves. The end result is a brighter life with her in it."

A man:
"Right now I don't know any. When you get the answer,

let me know."

Kato:
"This is a fictional character, but I'm going to say Monica from the movie *Love & Basketball*. The reason that I say this is because of her strength. She is a fighter, yet still learning to be a fighter. And when she loves her man... she goes all the way. She doesn't always make the right decisions in situations... but the feelings that she has when she loves a man are powerful.

"What's cool is that she continues to learn in the process. She was goal-oriented. Another thing about Monica that was a serious turn-on for me was that she was by no means fake... and she was always honest about how she felt about stuff. Plus... she's so damn cute as hell - the girl next door type of cute, the natural."

Elliot:
"Peaceful; logical thinker; critical thinker; spiritual; self-respect; dignity; pride; honest; passionate; compassionate; goal-attainer; loves all that Life offers - the good, bad and in-between."

V. Anthony:
"What comes to mind is conversation. I'm thinking of a woman I know and a time in our experience as friends when we talked for hours and never did she complain or ruin her God given beauty by frowning out of frustration or taking away from the aura that existed between us. I sat in admiration of her spirit, her reflection.

"She shared the hard times and the good times that she'd gone through. I loved her reaction to any compliment that I'd give her. I felt like an artist. My paintbrush was respect with a little hint of flirtation. She lives in a different state from me and I often wonder if the canvas of her beauty will ever be within my reach again.

"But regardless of that possibility, I believe she

will always know just how amazing I believe her to be. Her light shines brightly as a woman, a mother, and supportive friend. She is a song that I wish I could sing to the world and whenever given the chance, I'll let everyone know she's a helluva girl!"

Her Highness

Diagnosis

Do you have any of the following symptoms?

Feeling that you're not loved?
Feeling that you don't belong?
Feeling that people are laughing at you or talking about you?
Feeling unappreciated?
Feeling rejected?
Unable to concentrate?
Wanting to sleep all the time?
Wanting to get away from it all?
Feeling embarrassed or unnecessarily judged?

Is it Social Anxiety Disorder?
Attention Deficit Disorder?
Depression?
Bipolar Disorder?

Maybe you just:

Need a vacation!
Need to have some fun!
Need to have really good sex (perhaps all by yourself)!
Need to forgive someone!
Need to forgive YOURSELF!
Need to appreciate yourself!
Need to be more thankful of your Power Source!
Need to know that all women feel one or more of these symptoms at least once a week!

Why are we feeling so bad? Usually because we get caught up in looking for validation in things that are horribly insignificant! We're not fully appreciating the beauty of what we already have. We're not stopping to smell the roses!

Medication? Here's your first dose. Step up to your throne and watch those symptoms disappear. Lady, you need a crown – one worthy only of the Queen of the Universe.

Reality is the leading cause of stress amongst those who are in touch with it. - Jane Wagner, writer and director, from *The Search for Signs of Intelligent Life in the Universe*

THE QUEEN TAKES ON... SUICIDAL THOUGHTS

The thought that it's "a permanent solution to a temporary problem" is usually not enough to stop most people from considering suicide. Though the topic rarely comes up for public discussion, the fact is that a lot of us have contemplated suicide at least once. *At least.*

DO: Think of other times in your life when you felt like there was no hope and how you made it through that tough situation.

DON'T: Think that this is the end of the world for you. You will survive if you give yourself the chance.

DO: Trust your Power Source to provide a solution to your crisis. A perfect end to your troubles could be just moments away. Isn't it worth it to wait and see?

DON'T: Try to predict what can or will happen. Your Power Source, as the most powerful force of the Universe, has limitless ways to bring you through.

DO: Sleep on it. It's amazing what rest and a few insightful dreams can do for a troubled mind.

DON'T: Underestimate the power of sleep and rest. Staying awake in order to worry will only increase your stress and it won't guarantee a faster solution to the crisis.

DO: Call a specialized hotline. Every city has a number

to call where there are caring people waiting to listen to you.

DON'T: Assume that no one is available to listen to you. Even a stranger can be a great help.

DO: Call someone you trust to give you good advice or a comforting shoulder without judging you.

DON'T: "Cry wolf." If you make a habit of calling the same people, threatening suicide every time you have a crisis, they will stop making themselves available for help.

In the darkest hour the soul is replenished and given strength to continue and endure. - Heart Warrior Chosa

Share the Wealth

Question: What do you do to cheer yourself up?

"I listen to music from the 70's and dance around the house or write poetry." – *Rebecca*

"I call my support system (sister). I talk to God, I talk to my family, turn on some happy music and tell myself what I'm thankful for: food, clothing, shelter, a job." – *Lola*

"Listen to music, paint, watch a video, go for a walk, pray, [drink] a glass of juice, talk to a friend or relative, take a nice bath, nap, treat myself to a fresh salad or fruit." –*Anonymous artist*

"I say positive affirmations to myself like: *I'm happy; I'm beautiful; Today is a great day!*" – *Samantha*

"I sing or play happy music. I wonder, do I sing because I'm happy or am I happy because I sing?" – *Sunshine*

"I write… and write… and write some more." – *Michelle*

"Listen to oldies; look at old photo albums; help someone out, even if it is a small gesture; sing along to CD's as if I'm on stage or in a video; go out on a date with a guy who'll spoil me." – *Tahira*

"Sing loudly to Gloria Gaynor's *I Will Survive*." – *Terri*

"To cheer my self up I write, or shop (mostly for books)." – *SasseeDiva*

"Take time to relax or take a shower." – *Felicia*

Try this!

If you're like a lot of queens and the very thought of exercising makes you feel faint... turn your everyday activities into workouts.

-Take the stairs when you're only going up a few floors.

-At the mall, grocery store, or any place with a big parking lot, do not lazily wait for people pulling out of the closest parking spaces. Get a healthy stroll by taking the furthest available parking space. (Exception: if it is dark or unsafe, park close to an entrance.)

-Be more acrobatic during sex. Your partner will be really impressed and you'll work muscles you didn't even know you had!

-At home with time on your hands? Get up and dance! See page 210 for examples of songs to dance around to when you need a boost.

-Party! Go to a place where you can dance the night away. And then, dance the night away!

God made a very obvious choice when he made me voluptuous; why would I go against what he decided for me? My limbs work, so I'm not going to complain about the way my body is shaped. - Drew Barrymore, actress, director, producer

Know the Difference

There is a difference between saying, "I'm happy with my weight," and "I love my body."

"I'm happy with my weight" = I eat cookies, cake, potato chips, pie, fast food, ice cream, candy bars and anything else that I know is junk food.

"I love my body" = I feed myself REAL food. There is a reason that certain things are labeled "junk food" and I limit my intake of these because my health is important to me. My eating habits don't come from vanity, but a show of appreciation for Life.

There is such a thing as a voluptuous woman who loves her body! And just because a woman is thin and satisfied with her weight, does not mean that she is healthy and loving her body.

Companies who promote junk food and fast food are all sitting back waiting for you to hate yourself enough to spend money to keep yourself in a state of self-hatred. How many times have you been eating a bag of chips, a pint of ice cream, or a double cheeseburger thinking, "I am so bad. I shouldn't be eating this. This is going right to my thighs..." yet you finished the whole bag, pint or fast-food meal?

Know what's a trip? First, THEY get paid to shove junk food down your throat, then THEY get paid to make you feel bad for falling for their sly advertising. THEY make you feel inadequate by forcing unrealistic images and diet commercials into your psyche. THEY are keeping you confused. We can't let them do this to us!

A Queen is carefully selective and that includes the foods she eats. There is nothing "wrong" with the way you look. However, the queen has to be healthy in order to be effective. Your goal is good health – for YOUR sake – not to impress anyone else by your appearance (though as a healthy queen, others can't help but be impressed). With your newfound attitude, you'll automatically go through changes in the way you view yourself. What you didn't like about your body, you'll find wasn't so bad after all or was just something you made up out of a belief that you would never be good enough.

QUEEN'S RULE: I EAT THE RIGHT FOODS FOR MY MENTAL, EMOTIONAL AND PHYSICAL HEALTH.

I don't stress over my weight. I just date men who like a little curve in their swerve. - Tahira Chloe Mahdi, author

Mirror, Mirror

Why your inability to lose weight may not have anything to do with your eating habits

Take time to reflect on your life. Are you used to people criticizing you? Have you felt that you were overly criticized or judged by a family member? Have you been hurt or betrayed by someone close to you?

You may feel as if you've gotten over these issues, but your subconscious mind hasn't let them go. You may have heard the expression, "Grow a thick skin," when dealing with rejection or criticism. Your weight *is* that thick skin. It's an armor you subconsciously use to shield yourself against criticism, betrayal or other emotional wounds.

How can a Queen begin to see permanent weight loss results?

The weight, just like the emotional issue, has to be released. We need to examine our lives and take an honest look at what has hurt us in the past. It helps to acknowledge the people whom we feel hurt by and our feelings toward them. If we are harboring resentment against people and are frightened that we may be hurt in the same way again, our health will reflect these feelings in some way.

Where should a Queen begin?

For some Queens, professional help is the answer. Your weight is merely a symptom of an emotional problem. A psychiatrist, psychologist or experienced counselor can help you acknowledge specific issues so that you are clearer about what you are up against. Once you recognize what's really going on, you can take the proper steps to heal yourself.

If you think you can sort through your past by yourself (you're right, by the way), there are plenty of books available in the Self-Help section of your local bookstore or library.

Is there anything else that may help?
Just as we need to release the criticism that others project onto us, we need to release the criticism we project onto others. Be mindful of your own critical behavior. Refuse to hold those hurtful thoughts toward others (friends, strangers, neighbors, celebrities, family or foes) and free your mind from that negative pattern.

Get rid of clutter around you. This includes objects in your home AND harmful people. Useless things stored cause clutter in your brain, which leads to clutter in your body. Start letting things go, especially old hurts.

Don't *lose* unwanted weight… you might find it again. RELEASE IT!!

Sometimes you've got to let everything go – purge yourself… If you are unhappy with anything… whatever is bringing you down, get rid of it. Because you'll find that when you're free, your true creativity, your true self comes out. – Tina Turner, singer

Share the Wealth

Question: What foods make you feel good? Are there any that bring you down? Why or How?

"Going back to my southern roots and good southern comfort food... Chicken & dumplings usually does the trick." - *Terri*

"Back when I ate meat, it was horseradish on everything! Sliced roast beef... man, did it ever make me HOT. Now that I'm a vegetarian (notice NOT VEGAN, just not a meat eater), I'd say it's KIPPERS... something about the OILS I guess." - *Michelle*

"Salads and fruits are uppers. Cakes, cookies and desserts are uppers as instant gratification, but soon bring me down. I wonder if the bottom line is more psychological than physical - guilt above nutrition. And then... Friday night and a fifth of wiskey on the rocks makes this queen sparkle." - *Sunshine*

"CHOCOLATE, CHOCOLATE, CHOCOLATE makes me HAPPY! HAPPY! HAPPY! And a lil' sexy..." - *Rebecca*

"Salads, fruits, and juices . . . they are awesome, they really make me feel good inside and out." - *Anonymous artist*

"I notice that I always feel energized after a garden salad. Cereal makes me feel full and satisfies my sweet cravings with no junk food guilt - in other words, I feel like I've gotten a good bargain! On the flip side: too much sugar makes me paranoid. What'chu lookin' at?" - *Tahira*

"Chocolate, brownies, chocolate chip cookie dough ice

cream... [but] If I overeat, any food can bring me down."
- *Samantha*

"Foods that make me feel better are healthy foods, green salad with red or green peppers. And tomatoes - yum! Rum and Coke, also." - *Lola*

On the Royal Menu

No carbs? Puh-leez. Your body needs carbohydrates to function. They give you energy that you are supposed to be burning while getting proper exercise. Rice, pasta and bread taste good and complete a lot of meals. It's as simple as eating "good" carbs such as brown rice, whole-wheat pasta and wheat/whole grain bread. The taste isn't even as different as you'd think. Besides, it's worth getting used to.

People who have lost a lot of weight through certain diets or surgeries also added EXERCISE to their lives. That's no coincidence. The EXERCISE is what got the weight off. Everything else was just mental.

Don't cut carbs, cut JUNK!! This is worth praying about, though it is rarely a secret what junk food is and isn't. Don't be like the people suing the fast food industry over their health issues; take responsibility for your health and your life! You know better!

Do your research and learn about nutrition to see which foods are good for you and which ones you should consume in moderation.

Try this!

For one week... Every time you get thirsty, drink water - nothing else but water.

When you feel stressed and want to calm down, drink water instead of an alcoholic beverage.

When you need a quick pick-me-up, drink water instead of coffee or an energy drink.

When you just want something tasty, drink water instead of juice or soda.

Water works wonders! It keeps you from being dehydrated, aids in digestion, clears your skin, moisturizes your skin and hair, lessens dandruff and scalp irritations and cleanses your internal organs.

Improved health and lowered stress levels? How appropriate for the Queen of the Universe. Let's see how often you can do this "Water for a Week" to make yourself look and feel great!

I come from a family where gravy is considered a beverage.
- Erma Bombeck, journalist, humorist

The Whole World in Your Hands

Your vagina was made to be loved. It is a very important part of you.

Take care of it. Consult your gynecologist about hygiene and how to best take care of your most private body part. Even if you don't have health insurance, it is worth it to spend money every six months to make sure that everything is working the way it should. Pap smears and other tests make it possible to detect early signs of cancer or infection so that you can remain healthy. Also, many STDs can go undetected in women and you need to be sure that you aren't carrying one or sleeping with the person who gave it to you.

Keep it clean. You can use deodorant soap on your body, but use only moisturizing soap on your vagina because it is very sensitive. Your vagina is a self-cleaning organ and douching is best done at the end of your period (if you feel it is necessary). Excessive douching and use of feminine deodorizers makes you more susceptible to vaginal infections. If you think that your vagina has an unhealthy, unusual or strong odor, see a doctor! Your vagina is not supposed to smell bad. Showers are cool and to be taken daily, but take a bath at least once a week for a good soak. Adding a cup of Epsom salt to your bath will freshen and soothe you in more ways than one. Feminine sprays are best applied to the outside of your panties, as to not contact your sensitive inner vulva. Powders should only be applied to pubic hair – and very sparingly.

Don't wear it out. While on your quest to find lovers worthy of your time and majestic presence, it isn't necessary to try them all out in the sack. A simple "see n' touch test" will do, once you decide you like someone, to determine if you want to experience more of what you see and feel. Save "all the way" until you are sure that you want this person in some capacity. Even if you are with the fling thing, keep your one-night/short lived trysts few and far between. You owe your vagina only the best. Besides, you can always…

Masturbate. Your vagina is your own responsibility. In addition to keeping it clean, comfortable and exclusive, you should know how to make it feel good. Masturbation does more for you than fight the cravings of sex when you have no worthwhile prospects. It also helps relieve tension and headaches. A woman must be self-sufficient and know what makes her feel good. Learn your vagina and what makes it happy so that when you do find someone you'd like to have sex with, you can let that person know as well.

Love it. Unless you feel that you are a man living inside a woman's body (in that case, you're reading the wrong book), be thankful for your vagina. It's yours. Love it. A lot of men do and a lot of women do too. Why shouldn't you? Don't be angry that you got your period in the middle of your vacation or feel burdened that you can't urinate at any time and place like a man can. Negative feelings toward your vagina bring on bad PMS and other illnesses. There are very good reasons why your vagina works the way it does. Want to know some? Good! Research is always fun. There are tons of books and websites dedicated to the celebration of the vagina. Go find some!

Mirror, Mirror

How vaginal infections can give us the perfect excuse

All of our health problems come from particular thoughts we are holding on to and our body's way of attempting to get rid of them. In the case of those disheartening, annoying, frustrating vaginal infections, our bodies are reacting to our thoughts about sex. An infection can give us an excuse to not have sex or can make sex so unpleasant that it serves as a form of punishment.

Why would a woman need an excuse to not have sex?
In such instances, it is left to a woman's subconscious to stop sexual activity when she doesn't have the heart to say, "No." Women who have frequent vaginal infections are in some way uncomfortable with sex - or just sex with a particular person. Through counseling or careful introspection, a woman can work through sexual resentment and negative sexual issues from her past. She must also evaluate her current relationship(s) and decide if she is comfortable with her partner(s).

Why would a woman continue to have sex if it is uncomfortable?
A woman's subconscious may hold unhealthy beliefs about sex and can lead her to feel as if she deserves to be chastised for having sex. She endures the pain in order to please her partner and punish herself at the same time. Some women even believe (because they were taught so) that they are not supposed to enjoy sex and that they should always be accommodating to a man who wants sex.

What does the past have to do with current infections?
Sexual abuse of some sort is one reason that a

woman would have frequent infections. Sexual abuse includes rape, improper or unwelcome touching (suffered at any age and at the hands of anyone), and various forms of sexual harassment. When a woman has been violated, it goes way past physical trauma. Mental damage is always done.

Also, our parents can have a huge impact on how we view sex. Some parents, in an attempt to ensure their daughters' purity, literally scare them into a lifetime of uncomfortable sex and unhealthy attitudes toward the human body in general. If a woman has always seen her vagina as something dirty, it is difficult for her to have a healthy and happy sex life.

What if she was never abused and is happy with her current relationship?
A relationship that is not in a woman's best interest will impact her subconscious mind, even if her conscious mind is in denial. She may consciously disregard all warning signs that she should leave the relationship, but her subconscious mind never fails her. Her partner doesn't have to be abusive or dangerous; he may be inappropriate or undeserving. For example: If the relationship is one that she feels the need to keep secret, feelings of guilt will sustain vaginal infections.

Queens also might find themselves in relationships where everything is right except the sexual aspect of it. A woman often doesn't agree with her partner's sexual expectations. She may feel that he wants it too much or just in the wrong ways. The infections provide her with an excuse to say no, most of the time.

Are there any other reasons?
Our personal morals, religious beliefs, or feelings of pressure from society give us different ideas about sex.

Many people in this world believe that sex before marriage is wrong or that sex without a serious relationship is detestable – even if they, themselves, are engaging in such behavior. If you feel deep down that sex before marriage is wrong or that some aspect of your relationship is morally wrong, your internal conflict will cause something to go wrong in your body, namely infection or an STD.

In other cases, our feelings of frustration with different situations and circumstances can give us vaginal discomfort. Stress is a common cause of minor infections. Allowing ourselves to be calm or to release anxiety over an issue can relieve minor irritation we may experience from time to time.

QUEEN'S RULE: I RELEASE ALL GUILT. I AM FREE TO ENJOY SEX. I AM FREE TO ABSTAIN FROM SEX IF I CHOOSE. I DESERVE A HEALTHY VAGINA.

Share the Wealth

Question: Have you ever had an illness and realized that it was stress-related? Have you ever gotten over a sickness by changing something in your life (home, job, relationship, attitude)?

Samantha's victory:
"Acid Reflux Disease. I was stressing over a cheating, manipulative, mentally abusive man day after day. My chest began to burn as if someone lit a bonfire in my esophagus. The doctor diagnosed me with the disease and told me that whatever the stress is, I need to let it go. I did just that after constant prayer and withdrawals. I take better care of myself now and I try my best not to let others cause me pain, physically and mentally."

Rebecca's victory:
"Lord yes! When I was working two jobs and raising my husband's children by his first marriage, my blood pressure went up...when I made him get the weekend job and stop being such a perfectionist, my blood pressure returned to normal."

Sunshine's victory:
"Yes, my illness was constipation and depression. I got rid of the man, which cured the depression, which cleared my mind to seek better nutrition, which enlightened my thoughts to clear mental and physical clutter – body and home. It's funny how one step leads to the next towards perfect balance."

Lola's victory:
"Oh yeah! Living with a terrorist daily was like walking on eggshells. I always had my heart in my mouth, wor-

rying about what would set him off or upset him. It gave me chest pains. Going to the doctor, having what seemed like a heart attack, scared me enough to know that I had to change my life. After leaving Ol' Stinky Bastard... miraculously, the pains left. I wonder why. Girls, GET OUT!"

SasseeDiva's victory:
"All of my adult life I have been stressed out doing what other people wanted me to do. That's why NOW is MY time to do what I want to do."

Tahira's victory:
"When I was 13, I was diagnosed with Reflex Sympathetic Dystrophy, a form of childhood arthritis. A doctor concluded this only after I had gone to many doctors and specialists to find out why I had constant horrible pains in my left arm and leg. It was bad until I went to college and it has been coming and going since, but not as badly. Once I started to get more spiritually aware, I realized that the pains didn't start until after I moved out of an abusive home situation. I was so used to being in pain physically, mentally and emotionally, that I couldn't allow myself to be at peace. I was stuck in a victim mentality that kept me in pain just so I could get the sympathy I never got while I was being abused. I am now more aware of when I am allowing myself to be in pain and I can quickly eliminate the pain by eliminating the defeated victim's mindset."

Happily Ever After

Try this!

If you don't have a computer with a CD burner, find someone who does.

For between 79 - 99¢ per song, you can download your own theme songs from special websites and make your own Queen of the Universe CD! You probably have great theme music in your current collection that will do just fine.

Make the first Queen of the Universe CD especially for your own empowerment. Subsequent CDs can serve many other purposes. Here are some examples of Queen of the Universe CD themes and songs that can get you started.

To remind you why you left your ex and give you the motivation to move on
"My Lovin' (You're Never Gonna Get It)" by En Vogue
"All Cried Out" by Lisa Lisa and Cult Jam
"There You Go" by Pink
"Sin Wagon" by the Dixie Chicks

To boost your spirit and remind you of how great life is
"Spill the Wine" by War
"Groove Is In The Heart" by Deee-Lite
"Fantasy" by Earth, Wind & Fire

To remind you to have a good time and provide exercise music for when you dance around by yourself or with a friend
"Give It Away" by the Red Hot Chili Peppers
"Flashdance... What A Feeling" by Irene Cara
"Got to Give It Up" by Marvin Gaye
"YMCA" by Village People

To let out some steam when someone pisses you off
"Take It Personal" by Gang Starr
"Out ta Get Me" by Guns 'N Roses
"Back Stabbers" by The O'Jays
"Lost Ones" by Lauryn Hill

To remind you that you deserve only the best love life
"Love Me In a Special Way" by DeBarge
"Express Yourself" by Madonna
"A Rose is Still A Rose" by Aretha Franklin
"That Girl" by Stevie Wonder

To serenade you as you make those changes along your journey
"I'm Coming Out" by Diana Ross
"New Attitude" by Patti LaBelle
"Three Little Birds" by Bob Marley

Queen Theme Songs
"Video" by India.Arie
"Beautiful" by Christina Aguilera
"Control" by Janet Jackson
"Superbad" by James Brown

And don't forget the **"Love Yourself First" Queen Themes** on page 16.

Share the Wealth

Question: As Queen, if you could make rules for everyone to follow, what types of laws would you impose?

Queen Lola:
Listen to what I say! Each woman should have four men. Women are so complicated, usually. The average man cannot satisfy her needs and all her complicated matters <smile>. And the woman needs a good schedule.

Queen SasseeDiva's decree:
For everyone... MIND YOUR OWN BUSINESS!

Queen Rebecca's decree:
All men shall treat their mates as though they were their best friends.

People shall share equally in the nurturing of children and in the division of household chores.

Man on woman violence will be met with swift and strong justice.

Women shall be allowed two weeks a year to get away from family and responsibilities with Pay! Annually! (Not at the same time of course. The world would be a mess!)

Queen Sunshine's decree:
All people would have the power to see karma in motion. That way, religious institutions wouldn't have to use their theories to rule people. We could actually see ourselves getting our deeds back ten-fold, the good and the bad.

Anonymous Queen's decree:
Everyone would have to respect their fellow man, no matter where they ranked in life with money, brains, ethnicity and beauty.

Queen Dionne's decree:
Outlaw the word "bitch." Although some women can act like one and we use it very loosely, in its true form, the word "bitch" is very derogatory and demeaning to women, regardless of the context. (I refuse to give the word "bitch" power by capitalizing it).

The older men/women must guide, teach, and mentor the younger men/women. Most of our young people are lost simply because they don't have proper role models or have not had the opportunity to have a strong male/female presence in their lives.

For men and women: if you lie down and make a baby, you will get up and take care of it!

Men would be required to treat all women like royalty: Open my door! Escort me to my car! Walk on the outside of the sidewalk! Help me with my coat! Chivalry will be alive and well!

Queen Tahira's decree:
Children must be educated on the history of the world's religions and spiritual practices as a part of their schooling. They should be free to decide how to worship when they feel they are ready.

There is only one race: HUMAN.

Parents must read to their children every night from the time they are born until the time they are educated enough to read for themselves. At that time, children under age 18 must read for one hour every night before they go to bed – 11:00 on school nights if they're in high school.

Teachers and professional athletes... your salary ranges are switched!

The fashion and entertainment industries must reflect all people, all over the globe.

Queen Michelle's decree:
RULES OF LOVE:

NO LYIN'

NO CHEATIN'

NO BEATIN'

NO DEMEANIN'

NO HUMILIATIN'

NO BACK STEPPIN'

NO RENEGIN'

NO LEAVIN'

NO QUITTIN'

NO CRYIN' UNCLE

About **KINGS SPEAK**

When women want advice on how to deal with men, they usually ask other women. Though there are special things about which women have to educate each other, there are other questions that are best answered by men - especially when **they** are the subject at hand. I knew it would be a fun addition to *How to Be Queen of the Universe* for readers to get opinions from men who want to get along with women just as much as we want to get along with men.

The men were so passionate about the issues discussed and so eager to share their thoughts, that I didn't edit their responses to exclude profanity or things that a woman would view as insensitive or politically incorrect. If you want to hear something that will comfort you and validate your feelings, you need to talk to a woman. To hear an honest opinion - straight with no chaser - you need to talk to a man.

I sent emails, made phone calls, conducted tape-recorded interviews, solicited responses from Internet message boards and had in-person conversations in order to collect these answers. The same questions were asked to each man. Each man chose which of the questions he wanted to answer.

You may find it interesting that most of the men didn't want their locations, professions, ages, or ethnic backgrounds revealed. Seven of them didn't want their real names used and one responded simply by saying, "I'm a man, dammit!" when I asked him for personal information. I didn't mind because this book is for every woman, everywhere, and part of the goal is to encourage people to see everyone as an individual, regardless of society's categories of race and class. But I know you're curious, so here are a few facts about our male focus group:

The youngest man to respond was 21 at the time of his interview. The oldest was 43. One has gray hair but is under 35. I asked OLDER men for help, but they didn't take me seriously.

Respondents' professions include but are not limited to: project manager for the government; acclaimed author; Ph.D. candidate; daycare worker; police officer; musician; and computer geek of some kind. There are also two attorneys, two electricians, and two independent business owners (retail).

At the time of the interviews, three of the men were married; one was divorced; one was engaged; three were living with their girlfriends; eight were single, yet actively dating; the rest were in serious relationships.

All in all, it's a good mix of guys and I was surprised to see that the "raw and unpolished" nature of an answer didn't mean that the respondent was of a certain age, socio-economic status, geographical location, or ethnicity. The tone of an answer actually depended upon how strongly a man felt about a particular subject and not upon his level of education or any of the aforementioned factors.

The men, or Focus Group Kings as I call them, were very supportive in giving me their opinions and they genuinely treasured the opportunity to share their feelings with so many women. I appreciate the time, effort and honesty they gave in order to make this book something special for us.

About *Share the Wealth*

The focus group Queens come from all walks of life, all over the country. Some are divorced (once or twice), some are single, and some are married - a few for the second or third time. Two are grandmothers! I knew better than to print their ages (ranging from 21 to 51 at the time of the interviews). However, in appreciation for their contributions to this book, I'm including the following quotes on age.

It takes a long time to become young. - *Pablo Picasso, artist*

If the young knew and the old could, there is nothing that couldn't be done. - *Proverb*

The woman who tells her age is either too young to have anything to lose or too old to have anything to gain. - *Chinese proverb*

Don't you know WOMAN and AGE is a contradiction in terms? - *Michelle McGriff, novelist*

Time and trouble will tame an advanced young woman, but an advanced old woman is uncontrollable by any earthly force. - *Dorothy L. Sayers, author*

Age is whatever you think it is. You are as old as you think you are. - *Muhammad Ali, world renowned athlete and poet*

I'm not interested in age. People who tell me their age are silly. You're as old as you feel. - *Elizabeth Arden, beautician and businesswoman*

We grow neither better nor worse as we get old, but more

like ourselves. – *May L. Becker, writer*

It takes courage to grow up and turn out to be who you really are. - *E.E. Cummings, poet*

If a woman tells you she's 20 and looks 16, she's 12. If she tells you she's 26 and looks 26, she damn near 40. - *Chris Rock, comedian and actor*

Author's Thanks

Thank you, God, my Divine Guidance, my Infinite Wisdom, my Everlasting Love for everything, especially those lessons I need really, really badly.
Thank you, Mommy, for loving me, supporting me and being such an angel. I believe we choose our parents so let me take this time to pat myself on the back.
Thank you, Aunt Debbie (real mom), for all that you do. The food, the laughs, and *Club Miss* really enrich my life!
Thank you, Roc. I knew you'd come in handy one day.

Without the following people, this book wouldn't have been done with such fervor: Wendell Davis III and family, Louis M. Lopez, Jr. and family, Greg Ford, Kwesi Rollocks, Lynda Wade, Markam Haughton, Kenyetta McKinney, Michelle McGriff, Richard Holland, Kevin Neale, Dave Powell, Storm the Unpredictable, Elliott Cunningham, James Lisbon, Christopher H. Page, Mark T. Ward, Kevin Hammond, Preston Blue II, DeLano McRavin, Terri Teague, Patrick Hodges, and Dwayne Thomas

Thank you, Coretta (my sister, the Queen) for being THE VERY BEST and for letting me hang out with the fam. Thank you, Bennett, Lil Marv, Kaylee and Miss Cora for sharing.

Thank you, Dr. Youlanda Gibbons for all of your support! You give me more evidence of angels on Earth. I'm awed at your ability to uplift and inspire.

Thanks to my family: the Shorts; the Youngs; Uncle James Rock; David Towler; Vernoi, Randy and Verry Davis; Vanessa Blackwell; Chris Miller and family; Dorothy Dixon; Alexander Dixon and family; Kathleen Reynolds and family; the Buchanan/Smith/Hall family; Aunt Chloe McGrady

Thanks to my literary biz and entertainment industry

companions for their support and encouragement: Tinesha Davis, LaDawn Black, Reggie Saunders, Jay B. Scott, Damita Shaw, Finesse "The Best", C. Lorenzo Johnston, Valerie Casey, Artist C. Arthur, Tiffany Wade, Rabiyah Kincey, Nicole Stevenson, Crystal M. Ellis, V. Anthony Rivers, Cha Ross-Estes, Jonathan Luckett, Antonio Richardson, Sylvia L. Simmons, Gayle Jackson Sloan, Ashan R. Hampton, Samantha Luck, Karen Ruffin, Gary Johnson, Tee C. Royal, Monica Carter, Natalie Darden, Sonya Harris, Jessica Tilles, Tracy Press, Kenda Bell, Kristie Cameron, Nikki Turner, Greg Calloway, LaShun Beal, Rom Wills and Shawn Faulkner

Thanks also to: Marcus Sills, *Take Me Out to the GoGo* Magazine, *AMAG-Awareness* Magazine, *Grind Mode* Magazine, Kaisha Moss, Linda Washington-Johnson, Jackson Mississippi Readers Club, "Giant Steps HipHop Urban" TV (Elliott, Bilal, Bishara), Qualitees Plus (Security Mall, Baltimore), Jokes On Us Comedy Club, Karibu Books, Caravan Books (Oxon Hill), Dionne Curbeam, Elizabeth Broadway, Summer Dye Gallery, Akosua Crafts, The Wet August Company, LaReeta Robinson with Sistahs of Color Reading Group (Little Rock, Arkansas), Jeanette Cullum, Tony Alleyne, The Micology Family of CCBC Catonsville, Nancey Flowers, Lonna Hooks, Life Changes Book Club, Avatar Salon & Wellness Spa (Silver Spring), the Broadcasting Institute of Maryland (staff, students and alumni), Rita J. Walker, Glassmanor Elementary School, Edgar Allan Poe Elementary School, the community of Forest Heights, Mayor Paula R. Noble and my next door neighbors.

If you feel that I owe you some thanks, call me and I'll write your name in your copy right below this sentence...

To everyone I've ever known... If it weren't for you, I wouldn't have learned a thing! Thank you!

About the Author

Name: Tahira Chloe Mahdi

Resides in: Maryland (She's a native.)

Besides writing books: writes articles for entertainment-based magazines and websites, dabbles in radio and television work, takes lots of time to relax

Education: Morgan State University, the Broadcasting Institute of Maryland, lots of time watching people, some time listening to people whine, some time listening to herself whine, three years in radio, two years working at a comedy club, four years traveling the U.S. for booksignings and vacations and a life of days and nights spent reading EVERYTHING

Most proud of: her recipes and her mother

Always wanted to: write a few books, be in a few movies, write a few movies, be in an "all-girl" band

Loves to: cook, eat, flirt, quote

Would recommend: spending time alone, fresh fruit smoothies, an exciting single life before marriage

People assume that she likes: slow songs, poetry, sensitive men

Actually likes: getting massages, dancing, brilliant men

At all times: is thankful for what she has, prays that the Divine will be done

Hardly ever: takes herself too seriously